SAY IT IN ITALIAN

BY

OLGA RAGUSA

Professor of Italian
Columbia University

DOVER PUBLICATIONS, INC.

NEW YORK

Published in Canada by General Publishing Company, Ltd., 30 Lesmill Road, Don Mills, Toronto, Ontario.
Published in the United Kingdom by Constable and Company, Ltd., 10 Orange Street, London WC 2.

Standard Book Number: 486-20806-0

Manufactured in the United States of America
Dover Publications, Inc.
180 Varick Street
New York, N.Y. 10014

CONTENTS

INTRODUCTION

SAY IT IN ITALIAN makes available to you, in simple, usable form, the sentences and expressions you will need for travel and everyday living in Italy. The phrases given are those shown by experience to be the most needed. The translations are idiomatic rather than literal, since your primary goal is to make yourself understood. In order to achieve correct pronunciation, all the Italian words are presented in a simple phonetic transcription explained in the Scheme of Pronunciation.

SENTENCE STRUCTURE

No attempt is made in this book to teach Italian grammar; all the phrases are complete in themselves and may be used without a knowledge of grammar.

The framework is designed to help you form additional sentences of your own. Thus, for the words in square brackets you can substitute the words immediately following—in the same line or in the indented entries below. For example, the entry: "I am [hungry] thirsty," provides two sentences: "I am hungry," and "I am thirsty." Three sentences are provided by the entry:

> I am [a student].
> —— a teacher.
> —— a business man.

As your Italian vocabulary increases, you will find that you can express a wide range of thoughts by substituting the proper words in these model sentences.

Parentheses are used in this book for two purposes:

(1) To indicate words that may or may not be wanted in a sentence:

> I (do not) understand.

(2) To enclose explanatory matter:

> Zabaglione. Light dessert custard of egg-nog flavor (made of egg yolks, sugar, wine and served hot or cold).

GENDER

Do not be deterred from speaking Italian by the fact that you will undoubtedly make grammatical errors. A native listener will usually understand what you mean to say. However you can avoid many errors by paying due attention to the gender of nouns.

THE INDEX

You will find the extensive index at the end of this book especially helpful. All the sentences, phrases and words are numbered consecutively from 1 to 1858. Numbers in the index refer you to each specific entry. In addition each major section is capitalized and indexed in bold face according to page number.

The primary purpose of the index is of course to enable you to locate quickly the specific word or phrase you need at the moment. But it can do more for you. If you will compare the various passages in which the same word occurs, you will discover a great deal about its forms. You will also become aware of synonyms and otherwise related words.

PRONUNCIATION

Say It In Italian follows the standard language of Florence and Rome, the central part of Italy. When you travel in Italy, you will hear many dialectic differences and variations in native speech. But if you use the standard literary speech, you will be understood everywhere.

Pronounce the phonetic transcriptions as though they were English text, with due regard for those few Italian sounds that do not exist in English. Do not memorize the following table—though you would do well to read through it once. Try pronouncing half a dozen of the phrases, then check yourself by the table. You will quickly find that you have learned the scheme and need refer to the table only rarely.

SCHEME OF PRONUNCIATION

Letter	Transcription	Example	Notes
a	ah	as in *father*	
b	b	as in *bat*	
c	k or ch	as in *sky* or *church*	The *c* is pronounced *k* before *a, o, u,* or *h*. Before *e* or *i,* it is pronounced *ch.*
d	d	as in *dental*	Pronounced with tongue against the back of upper teeth.
e (open)	e or eh	as in *met*	
e (closed)	ay	as in *date*	Pronounce the closed *e* as one sound, not a diphthong. Practice by prolonging the sound of *ay* without permitting yourself to end on *ee.*
f	f	as in *fate*	
g	g or j	as in *go* or *joke*	The *g* is hard before *a, o, u,* or *h*. Before *e* or *i,* it is pronounced *j.*
h	silent		
i	ee	as in *feed*	
l	l	as in *let*	
m	m	as in *met*	
n	n	as in *net*	

Letter	Transcription	Example	Notes
o (open)	aw	as in *lawyer*	Pronounce the *o* as one sound, not as a diphthong. Practice by prolonging the sound of *o* without permitting yourself to end on *oo*.
o (closed)	o or oh	as in *notify*	
p	p	as in *spry*	
qu	kw	as in *quick*	
r	r	as in *ride*	The Italian *r* is trilled with the tip of the tongue.
s	s or z	as in *say* or *zeal*	
sci, sce	sh	as in *shell*	
t	t	as in *stop*	Pronounced with the tongue against the back of the upper teeth.
u	oo	as in *food*	
v	v	as in *zest*	
x	ks	as in *lacks*	
z	ts or dz	as in *lets* or *adze*	

Note: The *u* and *i* of Italian diphthongs *uo* and *ie* are represented by *w* and *y* respectively. For example: Buono (*BWAW-no*), lieto (*LYEH-toh*). Diphthongs written as REH_ee, LEH_ee, AH_oo are to be pronounced as one syllable with no break between the two vowel sounds.

THE ITALIAN ALPHABET

The Italian alphabet is given below along with the pronunciation of the name of each letter according to the transcription used in this book. You will find it useful in spelling out names and addresses.

Letter	Called	Letter	Called
A	ah	N	EN-nay
B	bee	O	o
C	chee	P	pee
D	dee	Q	koo
E	ay	R	EHR-ray
F	EF-fay	S	ES-say
G	jee	T	tee
H	AHK-kah	U	oo
I	ee	V	vee
J*	ee LOON-go	W*	DOHP-pyah vee
K*	KAHP-pah	X*	eeks
L	EL-lay	Y*	EEP-see-lohn
M	EM-may	Z	DZEH-tah

* The letters *j*, *k*, *w*, *x*, and *y* are not part of the Italian alphabet. They occur only in words and names of foreign origin.

GENERAL EXPRESSIONS
ESPRESSIONI COMUNI

1. Yes.
  Sì.
  see.

2. No.
  No.
  naw.

3. Perhaps.
  Forse.
  FOHR-say.

4. Please.
  Per favore.
  payr fah-VO-ray.

5. Excuse me.
  Mi scusi.
  mee SKOO-zee.

6. Thanks (very much).
  Grazie (tanto).
  GRAH-tsyay (TAHN-toh).

7. You are welcome.
  Prego.
  PREH-go.

8. It is (not) all right.
  (Non) va bene.
  (nawn) vah BEH-nay.

9. It doesn't matter.
  Non importa.
  nawn eem-PAWR-tah.

10. That is all.
Questo è tutto.
KWAY-sto eh TOOT-toh.

11. Wait a moment.
Aspetti un momento.
ah-SPET-tee oon mo-MAYN-toh.

12. Come in.
Avanti.
ah-VAHN-tee.

13. Come here.
Venga qui.
VEN-gah kwee.

14. What do you wish?
Che cosa vuole?
kay KAW-sah VWAW-lay?

15. What?
Che cosa?
kay KAW-sah?

16. Who?
Chi?
kee?

17. When?
Quando?
KWAHN-doh?

18. Where?
Dove?
DOH-vay?

19. Why?
Perchè?
payr-KEH?

20. How long?
Quanto tempo?
KWAHN-toh TEM-po?

21. How far?
Quant'è distante?
kwahn-TEH dee-STAHN-tay?

22. Listen!
Senta!
SEN-tah!

23. Look out!
Attenzione!
aht-ten-TSYOH-nay!

24. Look here.
Guardi.
GWAHR-dee.

YOURSELF

GENERALITÀ

25. I am an American citizen.
Sono cittadino americano.
SO-no cheet-tah-DEE-no ah-may-ree-KAH-no.

26. My name is John Smith.
Mi chiamo Giovanni Smith.
mee KYAH-mo jo-VAHN-nee "Smith."

27. I spell my name S M I T H.
Il mio nome si scrive *esse-emme-i-ti-acca.*
*eel MEE-oh NO-may see SKREE-vay ES-say EM-may
ee tee AHK-kah.*

28. I am [a student].
   Sono [studente] (masc.).
   SO-no [stoo-DEN-tay].

29. —— a student.
   studentessa (fem.).
   stoo-den-TAYS-sah.

30. —— a teacher.
   insegnante.
   een-say-NYAHN-tay.

31. —— a business man.
   uomo d'affari.
   WAW-mo dahf-FAH-ree.

32. I am here on [a business trip].
   Sono qui [per affari].
   SO-no kwee [payr ahf-FAH-ree].

33. —— a vacation.
   in vacanze.
   een vah-KAHN-tsay.

34. I am a friend of Mr. Silvi.
   Sono un amico del signor Silvi.
   SO-no oon ah-MEE-ko dayl see-NYOHR SEEL-vee.

35. My mailing address is 920 Broadway.
   Il mio recapito è 920 (nove cento venti) Broadway.
   eel MEE-o ray-KAH-pee-toh eh (NAW-vay CHEN-toh VAYN-tee) Broadway.

36. I am [hungry] thirsty.
   Ho [fame] sete.
   aw [FAH-may] SAY-tay.

37. I am [warm] cold.
   Ho [caldo] freddo.
   aw [KAHL-doh] FRAYD-doh.

38. I am [busy] tired.
Sono [occupato] stanco.
SO-no [ohk-koo-PAH-toh] STAHN-ko.

39. I am ready.
Sono pronto.
SO-no PROHN-toh.

40. I am in a hurry.
Ho fretta.
aw FRAYT-tah.

41. I am glad.
Sono contento.
SO-no kohn-TEN-toh.

42. I am sorry.
Mi dispiace.
mee dee-SPYAH-chay.

GREETINGS AND SOCIAL CONVERSATION

SALUTI E CONVENEVOLI

43. Good morning.
Buon giorno.
bwawn JOHR-no.

44. Good evening.
Buona sera.
BWAW-nah SAY-rah.

45. Hello.
Ciao.
CHYAH_o.

46. Good-bye.
Addio.
ahd-DEE-o.

47. I'll be seeing you.
Arrivederci.
ahr-ree-vay-DAYR-chee.

48. Until tomorrow.
A domani.
ah doh-MAH-nee.

49. How are you?
Come sta?
KO-may stah?

50. Fine thanks, and you?
Bene, grazie, e Lei?
BEH-nay, GRAH-tsyay, ay LEH_ee?

51. How is your family?
Come sta la sua famiglia?
KO-may stah lah SOO-ah fah-MEE-lyah?

52. (Not) very well.
(Non) molto bene.
(nawn) MOHL-toh BEH-nay.

53. How are things?
Come va?
KO-may vah?

54. All right.
Bene.
BEH-nay.

55. So, so.
Così, così.
ko-SEE, ko-SEE.

56. May I introduce [Mr.] Mrs., Miss ——?
Posso presentarle [il signor] la signora, la signorina ——?

PAWS-so pray-zayn-TAHR-lay [eel see-NYOHR] lah see-NYOH-rah, lah see-nyoh-REE-nah ——?

57. This is [my wife].
Questa è [mia moglie].
KWAY-stah eh [MEE-ah MO-lyay].

58. My husband.
Mio marito.
MEE-o mah-REE-toh.

59. My daughter.
Mia figlia.
MEE-ah FEE-lyah.

60. My son.
Mio figlio.
MEE-o FEE-lyoh.

61. My sister.
Mia sorella.
MEE-ah so-REL-lah.

62. My brother.
Mio fratello.
MEE-o frah-TEL-lo.

63. My mother.
Mia madre.
MEE-ah MAH-dray.

64. My father.
Mio padre.
MEE-o PAH-dray.

65. My child.
Il mio bambino (masc.).
eel MEE-o bahm-BEE-no.

66. My child.
La mia bambina (fem.).
lah MEE-ah bahm-BEE-nah.

67. My friend.
Il mio amico (masc.).
eel MEE-o ah-MEE-ko.

68. My friend.
   La mia amica (fem.).
   lah MEE-ah ah-MEE-kah.

69. Pleased to meet you.
   Piacere di fare la sua conoscenza.
   pyah-CHAY-ray dee FAH-ray lah SOO-ah ko-no-SHEN-tsah.

70. Excuse me, what is your name?
   Scusi, come si chiama Lei?
   SKOO-zee, KO-may see KYAH-mah LEH_ee?

71. Will you join us?
   Vuol tenerci compagnia?
   vwawl tay-NAYR-chee kohm-pah-NYEE-ah?

72. Sit down, please.
   Si accomodi, prego.
   see ahk-KAW-mo-dee, PREH-go.

73. Who is [that boy]?
   Chi è [quel ragazzo]?
   kee eh [kwayl rah-GAHT-tso]?

74. —— that man.
   quell'uomo.
   kwayl-LWAW-mo.

75. —— that woman.
   quella donna.
   KWAYL-lah DAWN-nah.

76. May I have your address and telephone number?
   Potrei avere il suo indirizzo e il numero del telefono?
   po-TREH_ee ah-VAY-ray eel SOO-o een-dee-REET-tso ay eel NOO-may-ro dayl tay-LEH-fo-no?

77. May I call on you again?
Posso venire a trovarla un'altra volta?
PAWS-so vay-NEE-ray ah tro-VAHR-lah oo-NAHL-trah VAWL-tah?

78. Come to see us.
Venga a trovarci.
VEN-gah ah tro-VAHR-chee.

79. I have enjoyed myself very much.
Mi sono divertito molto.
mee SO-no dee-vayr-TEE-toh MOHL-toh.

80. Regards to your aunt and your uncle.
Mi saluti sua zia e suo zio.
mee sah-LOO-tee SOO-ah DZEE-ah ay SOO-o DZEE-o.

81. I like you very much.
Mi è molto simpatico Lei (masc.).
mee eh MOHL-toh seem-PAH-tee-ko LEH_ee.

82. I like you very much.
Mi è molto simpatica Lei (fem.).
mee eh MOHL-toh seem-PAH-tee-kah LEH_ee.

83. I love you, dear.
Ti amo, cara (fem.).
tee AH-mo, KAH-rah.

MAKING YOURSELF UNDERSTOOD
FARSI CAPIRE

84. Do you speak English?
Parla inglese?
PAHR-lah een-GLAY-say?

85. Is there anyone here who speaks English?
C'è qualcuno qui che parla l'inglese?
cheh kwahl-KOO-no kwee kay PAHR-lah leen-GLAY-say?

86. I speak only English.
Parlo soltanto l'inglese.
PAHR-lo sohl-TAHN-toh leen-GLAY-say.

87. I know a little [Spanish].
Conosco un po' [lo spagnolo].
ko-NO-sko oon paw [lo spah-NYOH-lo].

88. —— French.
il francese.
eel frahn-CHAY-zay.

89. —— Italian.
l'italiano.
lee-tah-LYAH-no.

90. —— German.
il tedesco.
eel tay-DAY-sko.

91. Please speak (more) slowly.
Per favore parli (più) adagio.
payr fah-VO-ray PAHR-lee (pyoo) ah-DAH-jo.

92. I (do not) understand.
(Non) capisco.
(nawn) kah-PEE-sko.

93. Do you understand me?
Mi capisce?
mee kah-PEE-shay?

94. I (do not) know.
(Non) so.
(nawn) saw.

95. I (do not) think so.
(Non) mi pare.
(nawn) mee PAH-ray.

96. Repeat it, please.
Lo ripeta, per favore.
lo ree-PEH-tah, payr fah-VO-ray.

97. Write it, please.
Lo scriva, per favore.
lo SKREE-vah, payr fah-VO-ray.

98. What is that?
Che cos'è?
kay kaw-SEH?

99. What does that word mean?
Che cosa vuol dire quella parola?
kay KAW-sah vwawl DEE-ray KWAYL-lah pah-RAW-lah?

100. How do you say —— in Italian?
Come si dice —— in italiano?
KO-may see DEE-chay —— een ee-tah-LYAH-no?

101. How do you spell ——?
Come si scrive ——?
KO-may see SKREE-vay ——?

102. We need an interpreter.
Abbiamo bisogno d'un interprete.
ahb-BYAH-mo bee-ZO-nyo doon een-TEHR-pray-tay.

DIFFICULTIES
DIFFICOLTÀ

103. Where is [the American consulate]?
Dov'è [il consolato americano]?
doh-VEH [eel kohn-so-LAH-toh ah-may-ree-KAH-no]?

104. —— **the police station.**
la questura.
lah kway-STOO-rah.

105. —— **the lost and found office.**
l'ufficio degli oggetti smarriti.
loof-FEE-chyoh DAY-lyee ohj-JET-tee zmahr-REE-tee.

106. —— **the washroom.**
il gabinetto.
eel gah-bee-NAYT-toh.

107. —— **the men's room.**
il gabinetto per uomini.
eel gah-bee-NAYT-toh payr WAW-mee-nee.

108. —— **the ladies' room.**
il gabinetto per donne.
eel gah-bee-NAYT-toh payr DAWN-nay.

109. **Can you [help] me?**
Mi potrebbe [aiutare]?
mee po-TREB-bay [ah-yoo-TAH-ray]?

110. —— **tell me.**
dire.
DEE-ray.

111. **I am looking for my friends.**
Cerco i miei amici.
CHAYR-ko ee MYAY-ee ah-MEE-chee.

112. **I cannot find my hotel.**
Non riesco a trovare il mio albergo.
nawn RYEH-sko ah tro-VAH-ray eel MEE-o ahl-BEHR-go.

113. **I do not remember [the number] the street.**
Non ricordo [il numero] la strada.
nawn ree-KAWR-doh [eel NOO-may-ro] lah STRAH-dah.

114. I have lost [my purse].
Ho perduto [la borsetta].
aw payr-DOO-toh [lah bohr-SAYT-tah].

115. —— my wallet.
il portafogli.
eel pohr-tah-FAW-lyee.

116. It is (not) my fault.
(Non) è colpa mia.
(nawn) eh KOHL-pah MEE-ah.

117. I forgot [my money] my keys.
Ho dimenticato [il denaro] le chiavi.
aw dee-mayn-tee-KAH-toh [eel day-NAH-ro] lay KYAH-vee.

118. I missed my train.
Ho perduto il treno.
aw payr-DOO-toh eel TREH-no.

119. What am I to do?
Che cosa devo fare?
kay KAW-sah DAY-vo FAH-ray?

120. Where are we going?
Dove andiamo?
DOH-vay ahn-DYAH-mo?

121. Go away.
Se ne vada.
say nay VAH-dah.

122. I will call a policeman.
Chiamo una guardia.
KYAH-mo OO-nah GWAHR-dyah.

123. The money has been stolen from me.
Mi è stato rubato il denaro.
mee eh STAH-toh roo-BAH-toh eel day-NAH-ro.

124. Help!
Aiuto!
ah-YOO-toh!

125. Fire!
Fuoco!
FWAW-ko!

126. Thief!
Al ladro!
ahl LAH-dro!

TRAVEL: CUSTOMS
IN VIAGGIO: DOGANA

127. Where is the customs?
Dov'è la dogana?
doh-VEH lah doh-GAH-nah?

128. Here is [my baggage].
Ecco [il mio bagaglio].
EK-ko [eel MEE-o bah-GAH-lyoh].

129. —— my health certificate.
il mio certificato medico.
eel MEE-o chayr-tee-fee-KAH-toh MEH-dee-ko.

130. —— my identification paper.
la mia carta d'identità.
lah MEE-ah KAHR-tah dee-den-tee-TAH.

131. —— my passport.
il mio passaporto.
eel MEE-o pahs-sah-PAWR-toh.

132. —— **my landing card.**
il mio permesso di sbarco.
eel MEE-o payr-MAYS-so dee ZBAHR-ko.

133. **This [bag] valise contains gifts.**
Questa [borsa] valigia contiene dei regali.
*KWAY-stah [BOHR-sah] vah-LEE-jah kohn-TYEH-
nay day ray-GAH-lee.*

134. **The five pieces to your [left] right are mine.**
I cinque colli a sua [sinistra] destra sono miei.
*ee CHEEN-kway KAWL-lee ah soo-ah [see-NEE-
strah] DEH-strah SO-no MYAY-ee.*

135. **I cannot find all the baggage.**
Non riesco a trovare tutto il bagaglio.
*nawn RYEH-sko ah tro-VAH-ray TOOT-toh eel
bah-GAH-lyoh.*

136. **I have [nothing] something to declare.**
[Non] ho [niente] qualche cosa da dichiarare.
*[nawn] aw [NYEN-tay] KWAHL-kay KAW-sah
dah dee-kyah-RAH-ray.*

137. **Must I open everything?**
Devo aprire tutto?
DAY-vo ah-PREE-ray TOOT-toh?

138. **I cannot open the trunk.**
Non posso aprire il baule.
nawn PAWS-so ah-PREE-ray eel bah_OO-lay.

139. **These are all personal belongings.**
Sono tutti effetti personali.
SO-no TOOT-tee ayf-FET-tee payr-so-NAH-lee.

140. **There is only some clothing here.**
Qui c'è solo vestiario.
kwee cheh SO-lo vay-STYAH-ryoh.

141. Do I have to pay duty on these things?
　　Devo pagare dogana su questi oggetti?
　　*DAY-vo pah-GAH-ray doh-GAH-nah soo KWAY-stee
　　ohj-JET-tee?*

142. This is all I have.
　　Non ho che questo.
　　nawn aw kay KWAY-sto.

143. How much must I pay?
　　Quanto devo pagare?
　　KWAHN-toh DAY-vo pah-GAH-ray?

144. Have you finished?
　　Ha finito?
　　ah fee-NEE-toh?

BAGGAGE

BAGAGLI

**145. I want to leave these bags here for a few
days.**
　　Vorrei lasciare queste valigie qui per qualché
　　giorno.
　　*vohr-REH_ee lah-SHYAH-ray KWAY-stay vah-LEE-
　　jay kwee payr KWAHL-kay JOHR-no.*

146. Where is the baggage checked?
　　Dove si può depositare il bagaglio?
　　*DOH-vay see pwaw day-po-zee-TAH-ray eel bah-
　　GAH-lyoh?*

147. The baggage check.
　　Lo scontrino.
　　lo skohn-TREE-no.

148. The baggage room.
Il deposito bagagli.
eel day-PAW-zee-toh bah-GAH-lyee.

**149. Is it possible to check the baggage through
to —— on this ticket?**
Posso spedire il bagaglio per —— con questo
biglietto?
*PAWS-so spay-DEE-ray eel bah-GAH-lyoh payr ——
kohn KWAY-sto bee-LYAYT-toh?*

150. I wish to take out my baggage.
Vorrei ritirare il bagaglio.
vohr-REH_ee ree-tee-RAH-ray eel bah-GAH-lyoh.

151. Where can I find a porter?
Dove posso trovare un facchino?
DOH-vay PAWS-so tro-VAH-ray oon fahk-KEE-no?

152. What is your number?
Qual'è il suo numero?
kwah-LEH eel SOO-o NOO-may-ro?

153. Follow me, please.
Mi segua, per favore.
mee SAY-gwah, payr fah-VO-ray.

154. Be careful with this suitcase.
Stia attento a questa valigia.
STEE-ah aht-TEN-toh ah KWAY-stah vah-LEE-jah.

155. Put it all in a taxi.
Metta tutto in un tassì.
MAYT-tah TOOT-toh een oon tahs-SEE.

DIRECTIONS
INDICAZIONI

156. Can you recommend [a travel agent] a travel agency?

Mi può raccomandare [un agente di viaggi] un'agenzia di viaggi?

mee pwaw rahk-ko-mahn-DAH-ray [oon ah-JEN-tay dee VYAHJ-jee] oo-nah-JEN-tsee-ah dee VYAHJ-jee?

157. I want to go [to the airline office] to the Italian tourist office.

Vorrei andare [all'ufficio delle aviolinee] all'Ente Nazionale del Turismo.

vohr-REH_ee ahn-DAH-ray [ahl-loof-FEE-chyoh DAYL-lay ah-VYOH-lee-nay-ay] ahl-LEN-tay nah-tsyoh-NAH-lay dayl too-REE-smo.

158. Is the bus stop near here?

È qui vicino la fermata dell'autobus?

eh kwee vee-CHEE-no lah fayr-MAH-tah dayl-LAH_oo-toh-boos?

159. How long will it take to go to the airport?

Quanto ci vuole per andare all'aeroporto?

KWAHN-toh chee VWAW-lay payr ahn-DAH-ray ahl-lah_ay-ro-PAWR-toh?

160. When will we arrive at ——?

Quando si arriva a ——?

KWAHN-doh see ahr-REE-vah ah ——?

161. Is this the direct way to ——?

È questa la via diretta per ——?

eh KWAY-stah lah VEE-ah dee-RET-tah payr ——?

162. Please show me the way to go [to mid-town].
Per favore mi indichi la via per andare [in centro].
*payr fah-VO-ray mee EEN-dee-kee lah VEE-ah payr
ahn-DAH-ray [een CHEN-tro].*

163. —— to the shopping section.
al quartiere dei negozi.
ahl kwahr-TYEH-ray day nay-GAW-tsee.

164. —— to the residential section.
al quartiere residenziale.
ahl kwahr-TYEH-ray ray-see-dayn-TSYAH-lay.

165. Should I turn [to the east]?
Devo voltare [a est]?
DAY-vo vohl-TAH-ray [ah est]?

166. —— to the west.
a ovest.
ah AW-vayst.

167. —— to the north.
a nord.
ah nawrd.

168. —— to the right.
a destra.
ah DEH-strah.

169. —— to the left.
a sinistra.
ah see-NEE-strah.

170. —— at the traffic light.
al semaforo.
ahl say-MAH-fo-ro.

171. It is [on this side of the street], isn't it?
È [da questo lato della strada], non è vero?
*eh [dah KWAY-sto LAH-toh DAYL-lah STRAH-
dah], nawn eh VAY-ro?*

172. —— **on the other side of the boulevard.**
dall'altro lato del viale.
dahl-LAHL-tro LAH-toh dayl VYAH-lay.

173. —— **at the corner of the avenue.**
all'angolo del corso.
ahl-LAHN-go-lo dayl KOHR-so.

174. —— **beyond the bridge.**
al di là del ponte.
ahl dee LAH dayl POHN-tay.

175. —— **inside the station.**
nella stazione.
NAYL-lah stah-TSYOH-nay.

176. —— **outside the building.**
fuori dell'edificio.
FWAW-ree dayl-lay-dee-FEE-chyoh.

177. —— **opposite the city hall.**
dirimpetto al municipio.
dee-reem-PET-toh ahl moo-nee-CHEE-pyoh.

178. —— **beside the café.**
accanto al caffè.
ahk-KAHN-toh ahl kahf-FEH.

179. —— **in front of the statue.**
davanti alla statua.
dah-VAHN-tee AHL-lah STAH-twah.

180. —— **behind the school.**
dietro alla scuola.
DYEH-tro AHL-lah SKWAW-lah.

181. —— **straight ahead from the square.**
sempre avanti dopo la piazza.
*SEM-pray ah-VAHN-tee DOH-po lah PYAHT-
tsah.*

182. —— **in the middle of the circle.**
in mezzo all'incrocio.
een MED-dzo ahl-leen-KRAW-chyoh.

183. —— **forward.**
avanti.
ah-VAHN-tee.

184. —— **back.**
indietro.
een-DYEH-tro.

185. —— **in this direction.**
in questa direzione.
een KWAY-stah dee-ray-TSYOH-nay.

186. —— **in that direction.**
in quella direzione.
een KWAYL-lah dee-ray-TSYOH-nay.

187. **Is it near?**
È vicino?
eh vee-CHEE-no?

188. **How far is it?**
Quant'è lontano?
kwahn-TEH lohn-TAH-no?

189. **How does one go there?**
Come ci si va?
KO-may chee see vah?

190. **Can I walk there?**
Ci posso andare a piedi?
chee PAWS-so ahn-DAH-ray ah PYEH-dee?

191. **Which is the fastest way?**
Qual'è la via più breve?
kwah-LEH lah VEE-ah pyoo BREH-vay?

192. Am I going in the right direction?
Vado nella direzione giusta?
VAH-doh   NAYL-lah   dee-ray-TSYOH-nay   JOO-stah?

TICKETS
BIGLIETTI

193. Where is [the ticket window]?
Dov'è [lo sportello dei biglietti]?
doh-VEH [lo spohr-TEL-lo day bee-LYAYT-tee]?

194. —— the waiting room.
la sala d'aspetto.
lah SAH-lah dah-SPET-toh.

195. —— the information bureau.
l'ufficio informazioni.
loof-FEE-chyoh een-fohr-mah-TSYOH-nee.

196. How much is a [one-way] round trip ticket to ——?
Quant'è un biglietto di [andata] andata e ritorno per ——?
kwahn-TEH oon bee-LYAYT-toh dee [ahn-DAH-tah] ahn-DAH-tah ay ree-TOHR-no payr ——?

197. I want [a ticket].
Vorrei [un biglietto].
vohr-REH_ee [oon bee-LYAYT-toh].

198. —— a front seat.
un posto davanti.
oon PO-sto dah-VAHN-tee.

199. —— a seat near the window.
un posto vicino al finestrino.
oon PO-sto vee-CHEE-no ahl fee-nay-STREE-no.

200. —— a reserved seat.
un posto riservato.
oon PO-sto ree-sayr-VAH-toh.

201. —— a sleeper.
un posto in vagone letto.
oon PO-sto een vah-GO-nay LET-toh.

202. —— a compartment.
uno scompartimento.
OO-no skohm-pahr-tee-MAYN-toh.

203. —— a timetable.
un orario.
oon oh-RAH-ryoh.

204. I want to go [first] second class.
Voglio andare in [prima] seconda classe.
VAW-lyoh ahn-DAH-ray een [PREE-mah] say-KOHN-dah KLAHS-say.

205. Can I get something to eat on this trip?
Potrò trovare qualche cosa da mangiare in viaggio?
po-TRAW tro-VAH-ray KWAHL-kay KAW-sah dah mahn-JAH-ray een VYAHJ-jo?

206. May I stop at ——?
Posso fermarmi a ——?
PAWS-so fayr-MAHR-mee ah ——?

207. Can I go by way of ——?
Posso andare via ——?
PAWS-so ahn-DAH-ray VEE-ah ——?

208. How long is this ticket valid?
Per quanto tempo è valido questo biglietto?
payr KWAHN-toh TEM-po eh VAH-lee-doh KWAY-sto bee-LYAYT-toh?

209. How much baggage may I take?
  Quanto bagaglio posso portare?
  KWAHN-toh bah-GAH-lyoh PAWS-so pohr-TAH-ray?

AIRPLANE
IN AEREO

210. Is there bus service to the airport?
  C'è servizio di autobus per l'aeroporto?
  cheh sayr-VEE-tsyoh dee AH_oo-toh-boos payr lah_ay-ro-PAWR-toh?

211. At what time will they call for me?
  A che ora mi verranno a prendere?
  ah kay O-rah mee vayr-RAHN-no ah PREN-day-ray?

212. When is there a flight to ——?
  Quando c'è un aeroplano per ——?
  KWAHN-doh cheh oon ah_ay-ro-PLAH-no payr ——?

213. What is the flight number?
  Qual'è il numero del volo?
  kwah-LEH eel NOO-may-ro dayl VO-lo?

214. I (do not) have a confirmed reservation.
  (Non) ho un posto riservato.
  (nawn) aw oon PO-sto ree-sayr-VAH-toh.

215. Will they serve something to eat on the plane?
  Daranno da mangiare in aereo?
  dah-RAHN-no dah mahn-JAH-ray een ah_EH-ray-o?

216. How many kilos may I take?
  Quanti chili posso portare?
  KWAHN-tee KEE-lee PAWS-so pohr-TAH-ray?

217. How much must I pay per kilo for excess baggage?
Quanto si paga al chilo per il peso in eccesso?
KWAHN-toh see PAH-gah ahl KEE-lo payr eel PAY-so een aych-CHES-so?

BOAT

IN PIROSCAFO

218. Bon voyage!
Buon viaggio!
bwawn VYAHJ-jo!

219. All aboard!
A bordo!
ah BOHR-doh!

220. Is it time to go on board?
È tempo di salire a bordo?
eh TEM-po dee sah-LEE-ray ah BOHR-doh?

221. Can I take the ferry-boat to ——?
Posso prendere il ferry-boat per ——?
PAWS-so PREN-day-ray eel "ferry-boat" payr ——?

222. When is the next departure?
Quand'è la prossima partenza?
kwahn-DEH lah PRAWS-see-mah pahr-TEN-tsah?

223. Can I land at ——?
Posso sbarcare a ——?
PAWS-so sbahr-KAH-ray ah ——?

224. Please prepare my berth.
Per favore, mi prepari il letto.
payr fah-VO-ray, mee pray-PAH-ree eel LET-toh.

225. Open the porthole.
Apra l'oblò.
AH-prah lo-BLAW.

226. I want to rent a deck chair.
Vorrei noleggiare una sedia a sdraio.
vohr-REH_ee no-layj-JAH-ray OO-nah SEH-dyah ah
SDRAH-yo.

227. Where can I find [the purser]?
Dove posso trovare [il commissario di bordo]?
DOH-vay PAWS-so tro-VAH-ray [eel kohm-mees-SAH-
ryoh dee BOHR-doh]?

228. —— the steward.
il cameriere.
eel kah-may-RYEH-ray.

229. —— the cabin steward.
il cameriere.
eel kah-may-RYEH-ray.

230. —— the captain.
il capitano.
eel kah-pee-TAH-no.

231. I am going to [my cabin].
Vado [in cabina].
VAH-doh [een kah-BEE-nah].

232. —— the upper deck.
sul ponte superiore.
sool POHN-tay soo-pay-RYOH-ray.

233. —— the lower deck.
sul ponte inferiore.
sool POHN-tay een-fay-RYOH-ray.

234. —— on the dock.
sulla banchina.
SOOL-lah bahn-KEE-nah.

235. I feel seasick.
Ho il mal di mare.
aw eel mahl dee MAH-ray.

236. Do you have some bonamine?
Ha della bonamina?
ah DAYL-lah bo-nah-MEE-nah?

237. The lifeboat.
La barca di salvataggio.
lah BAHR-kah dee sahl-vah-TAHJ-jo.

238. The life preserver.
Il salvagente.
eel sahl-vah-JEN-tay.

TRAIN
IN TRENO

239. The arrival.
L'arrivo.
lahr-REE-vo.

240. The departure.
La partenza.
lah pahr-TEN-tsah.

241. Where is the railroad station?
Dov'è la stazione ferroviaria?
doh-VEH lah stah-TSYOH-nay fayr-ro-VYAH-ryah?

242. Where does one take the train for ——?
Dove si prende il treno per ——?
DOH-vay see PREN-day eel TREH-no payr ——?

243. When does the train for —— leave?
Quando parte il treno per ——?
KWAHN-doh PAHR-tay eel TREH-no payr ——?

244. Is the train from —— [late] on time?
È [in ritardo] in orario il treno da ——?
eh [een ree-TAHR-doh] een o-RAH-ryoh eel TREH-no dah ——?

245. My train leaves in ten minutes.
Il mio treno parte fra dieci minuti.
eel MEE-o TREH-no PAHR-tay frah DYEH-chee mee-NOO-tee.

246. From what [platform] gate, track does the train leave?
Da quale [marciapiede] cancello, binario parte il treno?
dah KWAH-lay [mahr-chyah-PYEH-day] kahn-CHEL-lo, bee-NAH-ryoh PAHR-tay eel TREH-no?

247. Does the train stop at ——?
Si ferma a —— il treno?
see FAYR-mah ah —— eel TREH-no?

248. How long does the train stop at ——?
Quanto tempo si ferma a —— il treno?
KWAHN-toh TEM-po see FAYR-mah ah —— eel TREH-no?

249. Can I get [an express] a local to ——?
Posso prendere un treno [rapido] accellerato per ——?
PAWS-so PREN-day-ray oon TREH-no [RAH-pee-doh] ahch-chayl-lay-RAH-toh payr ——?

250. Is there [a later] an earlier train?
    C'è un treno [più tardi] più presto?
    *cheh oon TREH-no [pyoo TAHR-dee] pyoo PREH-
       sto?*

251. Please [open] close the window.·
    Per favore [apra] chiuda il finestrino.
    *payr fah-VO-ray [AH-prah] KYOO-dah eel fee-nay-
       STREE-no.*

252. Where is [the dining car]?
    Dov'è [il vagone ristorante]?
    doh-VEH [eel vah-GO-nay ree-sto-RAHN-tay].

253. —— the baggage car.
        il bagagliaio.
        eel bah-gah-LYAH-yoh.

254. —— the smoking car.
        la carrozza per fumatori.
        lah kahr-RAWT-tsah payr foo-mah-TOH-ree.

255. —— the sleeper.
        il vagone letti.
        eel vah-GO-nay LET-tee.

256. Is this seat taken?
    Questo posto è occupato?
    KWAY-sto PO-sto eh ohk-koo-PAH-toh?

257. May I smoke?
    Posso fumare?
    PAWS-so foo-MAH-ray?

BUS, STREETCAR AND SUBWAY

IN AUTOBUS, TRANVAI E METRO-POLITANA

258. What [bus] streetcar, subway do I take to go to ——?

Quale [autobus] tranvai, metropolitana si prende per andare a ——?

KWAH-lay [AH̲_oo-toh-boos] trahn-VAH-ee, may-tro-po-lee-TAH-nah see PREN-day payr ahn-DAH-ray ah ——?

259. How much is [the fare] a transfer?

Quanto costa [il biglietto] un biglietto di coincidenza?

KWAHN-toh KAW-stah [eel bee-LYAYT-toh] oon bee-LYAYT-toh dee ko-een-chee-DEN-tsah?

260. Where does the bus for —— stop?

Dove si ferma l'autobus per ——?

DOH-vay see FAYR-mah LAH̲_oo-toh-boos payr ——?

261. Driver, do you go near ——?

Conduttore, lei passa vicino a ——?

kohn-doot-TOH-ray, LEH̲_ee PAHS-sah vee-CHEE-no ah ——?

262. Will I have to change?

Devo cambiare?

DAY-vo kahm-BYAH-ray?

263. Please tell me where to get off.

Per favore mi dica dove devo scendere.

payr fah-VO-ray mee DEE-kah DOH-vay DAY-vo SHAYN-day-ray.

264. I want to get off at the next stop.
Vorrei scendere alla prossima fermata.
vohr-REH_ee SHAYN-day-ray AHL-lah PRAWS-see-mah fayr-MAH-tah.

TAXI
IN TASSÌ

265. Please call a taxi for me.
Per favore mi chiami un tassì.
payr fah-VO-ray mee KYAH-mee oon tahs-SEE.

266. Are you free?
È libero?
eh LEE-bay-ro?

267. What do·you charge per [hour] kilometer?
Quanto prende [all'ora] al kilometro?
KWAHN-toh PREN-day [ahl-LO-rah] ahl kee-LAW-may-tro?

268. How much will the ride cost?
Quanto costa la corsa?
KWAHN-toh KAW-stah lah KOHR-sah?

269. I would like to take a tour around the city for one hour.
Mi piacerebbe girare per la città per un ora.
mee pyah-chay-REB-bay jee-RAH-ray payr lah CHEET-tah payr oon Ò-rah.

270. Please drive [more slowly].
Per favore vada [più adagio].
payr fah-VO-ray VAH-dah [pyoo ah-DAH-jo].

271. Please be careful.
Per favore faccia attenzione.
payr fah-VO-ray FAHCH-chyah aht-tayn-TSYOH-nay.

272. Can you stop here?
Può fermarsi qui?
pwaw fayr-MAHR-see kwee?

273. Please wait for me.
Per favore mi aspetti.
payr fah-VO-ray mee ah-SPET-tee.

AUTOMOBILE TRAVEL
IN AUTOMOBILE

274. Where can I rent [a car]?
Dove posso noleggiare [una macchina]?
DOH-vay   PAWS-so   no-layj-JAH-ray   [OO-nah MAHK-kee-nah]?

275. —— a motorcycle.
una motocicletta.
OO-nah mo-toh-chee-KLAYT-tah.

276. —— a motor scooter.
uno scooter.
OO-no SKOO-tayr.

277. I have an international driver's license.
Ho la patente internazionale di guida.
aw lah pah-TEN-tay een-tayr-nah-tsyoh-NAH-lay dee GWEE-dah.

278. What [town] is this?
Che [paese] è questo?
kay [pah-AY-zay] eh KWAY-sto?

279. —— village.
villaggio.
veel-LAHJ-jo.

280. —— city.
città.
cheet-TAH.

281. —— suburb.
sobborgo.
sohb-BOHR-go.

282. The next one.
La prossima.
lah PRAWS-see-mah.

283. Where does that road go?
Dove porta quella strada?
DOH-vay PAWR-tah KWAYL-lah STRAH-dah?

284. Is the road [rough]?
È [accidentata] la strada?
eh [ahch-chee-dayn-TAH-tah] lah STRAH-dah?

285. —— smooth.
liscia.
LEE-shah.

286. —— paved.
asfaltata.
ah-sfahl-TAH-tah.

287. —— in bad condition.
in cattivo stato.
een kaht-TEE-vo STAH-toh.

288. —— in good condition.
in buono stato.
een BWAW-no STAH-toh.

289. Can you show it to me on the road map?
Me lo può mostrare sulla carta automobilistica?
*may lo pwaw mo-STRAH-ray SOOL-lah KAHR-tah
ah_oo-toh-mo-bee-LEE-stee-kah?*

290. Where can I find [a gas station] a garage?

Dove posso trovare [un distributore di benzina] un'autorimessa?

DOH-vay PAWS-so tro-VAH-ray [oon dee-stree-boo-TOH-ray dee bayn-DZEE-nah] oo-nah-oo-toh-ree-MAYS-sah?

291. The tank is [empty] full.

Il serbatoio è [vuoto] pieno.

eel sayr-bah-TOH-yoh eh [VWAW-toh] PYEH-no.

292. How much is gas per liter?

Quanto costa la benzina al litro?

KWAHN-toh KAW-stah lah bayn-DZEE-nah ahl LEE-tro?

293. Give me twelve liters.

Me ne dia dodici litri.

may nay DEE-ah DOH-dee-chee LEE-tree.

294. Please change the oil.

Per favore cambi l'olio.

payr fah-VO-ray KAHM-bee LAW-lyoh.

295. [Light] medium, heavy oil.

Olio [leggero] medio, pesante.

AW-lyoh [layj-JEH-ro] MEH-dyoh, pay-SAHN-tay.

296. Put some water in the battery.

Metta dell'acqua nella batteria.

MET-tah dayl-LAHK-kwah NAYL-lah baht-tay-REE-ah.

297. Recharge the battery.

Ricarichi la batteria.

ree-KAH-ree-kee lah baht-tay-REE-ah.

298. Lubricate the car.

Lubrifichi la macchina.

loo-BREE-fee-kee lah MAHK-kee-nah.

299. Could you wash it [now] soon?
La può lavare [ora] al più presto?
lah pwaw lah-VAH-ray [O-rah] ahl pyoo PREH-sto?

300. I wish to leave my car here for the night.
Vorrei lasciare la macchina qui per la notte.
*vohr-REH_ee lah-SHYAH-ray lah MAHK-kee-nah
kwee payr lah NAWT-tay.*

301. Can you recommend a good mechanic?
Mi può raccomandare un buon meccanico?
*mee pwaw rahk-ko-mahn-DAH-ray oon bwawn mayk-
KAH-nee-ko?*

302. Adjust the brakes.
Verifichi i freni.
vay-REE-fee-kee ee FRAY-nee.

303. Check the tires.
Verifichi le gomme.
vay-REE-fee-kee lay GOHM-may.

304. Can you repair [a puncture] a flat tire?
Può riparare [una bucatura] una gomma a terra?
*pwaw ree-pah-RAH-ray [OO-nah boo-kah-TOO-rah]
OO-nah GOHM-mah ah TEHR-rah?*

305. The motor overheats.
Il motore riscalda troppo.
eel mo-TOH-ray ree-SKAHL-dah TRAWP-po.

306. The engine [misses] stalls.
Il motore [perde dei colpi] si spenge.
*eel mo-TOH-ray [PEHR-day day KOHL-pee] see
SPEN-jay.*

307. The motor rumbles.
Il motore sgrana.
eel mo-TOH-ray ZGRAH-nah.

308. There is [a rattling noise].
C'è [un ciottolío].
cheh [oon chyoht-toh-LEE-o].

309. —— a slight leak.
una piccola perdita.
OO-nah PEEK-ko-lah PEHR-dee-tah.

310. May I park here for a few hours?
Posso parcare qui per qualche ora?
*PAWS-so pahr-KAH-ray kwee payr KWAHL-kay
O-rah?*

HELP ON THE ROAD
RICHIESTA DI SOCCORSI

311. I am sorry to trouble you.
Mi dispiace di disturbarla.
mee dee-SPYAH-chay dee dee-stoor-BAHR-lah.

312. My car has broken down.
La mia automobile è in panna.
*lah MEE-ah ah͜_oo-to-MAW-bee-lay eh een PAHN-
nah.*

313. Can you help me move it out of traffic?
Mi può aiutare a spingerla fuori del traffico?
*mee pwaw ah-yoo-TAH-ray ah SPEEN-jayr-lah
FWAW-ree dayl TRAHF-fee-ko?*

314. Can you [push] tow the car?
Può [spingere] rimorchiare la macchina?
*pwaw [SPEEN-jay-ray] ree-mohr-KYAH-ray lah
MAHK-kee-nah?*

315. Can you help me change a tire?
Mi potrebbe aiutare a cambiare una gomma?
mee po-TREB-bay ah-yoo-TAH-ray ah kahm-BYAH-ray OO-nah GOHM-mah?

316. Could you lend me the jack?
Mi potrebbe prestare il cricco?
mee po-TREB-bay pray-STAH-ray eel KREEK-ko?

317. My car is stuck in [the mud] the ditch.
La mia macchina si è incagliata [nel fango] nel fossato.
lah MEE-ah MAHK-kee-nah see eh een-kah-LYAH-tah [nayl FAHN-go] nayl fos-SAH-toh.

318. Could you take me to a garage?
Mi potrebbe portare ad un autorimessa?
mee po-TREB-bay pohr-TAH-ray ahd oon ah_oo-toh-ree-MAYS-sah?

PARTS OF THE CAR
PARTI DELL'AUTOMOBILE

319. The accelerator. L'acceleratore.
lahch-chay-lay-rah-TOH-ray.

320. The battery. La batteria.
lah baht-tay-REE-ah.

321. The bolt. Il bullone. *eel bool-LO-nay.*

322. The brake. Il freno. *eel FRAY-no.*

323. The clutch. La frizione. *lah free-TSYOH-nay.*

324. The engine.   Il motore.   *eel mo-TOH-ray.*

325. The gear shift.   La leva del cambio.
lah LEH-vah dayl KAHM-byoh.

326. The headlight.   Il faro.   *eel FAH-ro.*

327. The horn.   Il clacson.   *eel KLAHK-sohn.*

328. The nut.   Il dado.   *eel DAH-doh.*

329. The spark plugs.   Le candele.
lay kahn-DAY-lày.

330. The spring.   La molla.   *lah MAWL-lah.*

331. The starter.   L'avviamento.
lahv-vyah-MAYN-ìoh.

332. The steering wheel.   Il volante.
eel vo-LAHN-tay.

333. The tail light.   Il fanalino posteriore.
eel fah-nah-LEE-no po-stay-RYOH-ray.

334. The tire.   La gomma.   *lah GOHM-mah.*

335. The spare tire.   La gomma di ricambio.
lah GOHM-mah dee ree-KAHM-byoh.

336. The wheel.   La ruota.   *lah RWAW-tah.*

337. The windshield wiper.   Il tergicristallo.
eel tayr-jee-kree-STAHL-lo.

TOOLS AND EQUIPMENT
ARNESI E MATERIALE VARIO

338. The chains.   Le catene da neve.
lay kah-TAY-nay dah NAY-vay.

339. The hammer.   Il martello.   *eel mahr-TEL-lo.*

340. The jack. Il cricco. *eel KREEK-ko.*

341. The pliers. Le tanaglie. *lay tah-NAH-lyay.*

342. The rope. La fune. *lah FOO-nay.*

343. The screwdriver. Il cacciavite.
eel kahch-chyah-VEE-tay.

344. The tire pump. La pompa.
lah POHM-pah.

345. The wrench. La chiave inglese.
lah KYAH-vay een-GLAY-say.

ROAD SIGNS
SEGNALAZIONI STRADALI

To facilitate the reading of road signs this section has been alphabetized in Italian and is followed by the comparable English translation.

346. Arrestarsi all'incrocio (Alt). Stop.

347. Attenzione! Caution!

348. Attenzione ai treni. Railroad crossing.

349. Attenzione al tranvai. Caution! Tramway.

350. Attenzione! Lavori in corso.
Caution! Construction ahead.

351. Attenzione nel sorpassare. Overtake with caution.

352. Cambiare marcia. Change gear.

353. Cambio di pista. Change lane.

354. Circolazione in senso opposto. Two-way traffic.

355. Circolazione vietata. Closed to all vehicles.

356. Cunetta. Bump; dip.

357. Curva e controcurva. Double curve.

358. Curva (pericolosa). (Dangerous) curve.

359. Curva stretta. Sharp turn.

360. Dare la precedenza sulle strade principali.
Major road ahead.

361. Deviazione. Detour.

362. Diritto o voltare a (destra) sinistrà.
Straight ahead or (right) left turn.

363. Discesa pericolosa. Steep grade.

364. **Divieto di parcheggio.** Parking prohibited.
365. **Divieto di segnalazioni acustiche.** Signaling prohibited.
366. **Divieto di sorpasso.** No passing; no overtaking.
367. **Divieto di sosta.** No parking.
368. **Dogana.** Customs.
369. **Entrata.** Entrance; entry.
370. **Fine dell'autostrada.** End of road.
371. **Frana.** Fallen rock.
372. **Gabinetti.** Toilets.
373. **Incrocio.** Crossroads; intersection.
374. **Incrocio pericoloso.** Dangerous junction.
375. **Incrocio precedenza.** Crossing main thoroughfare.
376. **Lavori in corso.** Road repairs.
377. **Limitazione altezza.** Height maximum.
378. **Limitazione di peso (larghezza).** Weight (width) limit.
379. **Limitazione di velocità.** Speed limit.
380. **Parcheggio libero.** Free parking.
381. **Passaggio a livello.** Level crossing.
382. **Passaggio a livello (custodito) incustodito.**
     (Guarded) unguarded crossing.
383. **Passaggio per pedoni.** Pedestrian crossing.
384. **Passerella.** Ferry.
385. **Per ciclisti.** Cyclists.
386. **Pericolo.** Danger.
387. **Pericolo di slittamento.** Icy in cold weather.
388. **Pista ciclabile incrocia.** Bicycle crossing.
389. **Posteggio.** Parking.
390. **Pregasi di ——.** You are requested to ——.
391. **Pronto soccorso.** First-aid station.
392. **Proprietà privata.** Private property.
393. **Rallentare.** Slow down.
394. **Rifornimento benzina.** Filling station.
395. **Senso obbligatorio a (destra) sinistra.**
     Keep (right) left.
396. **Senso obbligatorio diritto.** No turns.
397. **Senso proibito.** No entrance.
398. **Senso unico. (Divieto d'ingresso.)**
     One-way. (Do not enter.)
399. **Sottopassaggio.** Underpass.
400. **Stazione di servizio.** Service station.
401. **Stazione Merci.** Freight station.
402. **Strada a senso unico.** Entry to one-way street.

403. Strada gelata.   Icy road.
404. Strada malsicura.   Rough road.
405. Strada nazionale.   Main road.
406. Strada sdrucciolevole.   Slippery road.
407. Strada stretta.   Narrow road.
408. Tenere la (destra) sinistra.
    Keep to (right) left of sign.
409. Traffico circolare.   Rotating traffic.
410. Uscita.   Exit.
411. Velocità massima.   Limit speed.
412. Velocità normale.   Resume speed.
413. Velocità ridotta.   Drive slowly.
414. Vicolo cieco.   Dead end.
415. Vietato automobili (giorni festivi).
    Automobiles prohibited (on Sundays and holidays).
416. Vietato fermarsi.   Do not stop.   Keep going.
417. Vietato il transito.   No thoroughfare.
418. Vietato il transito ai motocicli.   Motorcycles prohibited.

PUBLIC NOTICES AND SIGNS
AVVISI E INSEGNE

This section has been alphabetized in Italian to facilitate the tourist's reading of signs.

419. Abbigliamenti per (signora) signori.
    (Ladies') men's clothing.
420. Affittasi camera ammobigliata.   Furnished room to let.
421. Affittasi (casa).   House for rent.
422. Agente di cambio.   Stockbroker.
423. Agente pubblicitario.   Advertising agent.
424. Agenzia di collocamento.   Employment agency.
425. Agenzia di trasporti.   Trucking.
426. Agenzia di viaggio.   Travel agency.
427. Ai piani superiori.   To the upper floors.
428. Ai treni.   To the trains.
429. Alloggio.   Room for rent.
430. All'imbarcazione.   To the boats.
431. Ambulanza.   Ambulance.
432. Amministrazione.   Manager's office.   (Management).
433. Antiquario.   Antiques.

434. Aperto dalle —— alle ——. Open from —— to ——.
435. Apparecchi (elettrici) radio. (Electrical) radio appliances.
436. Aria condizionata. Air conditioned.
437. Arredamenti. House furnishings.
438. Arrivo. Arrival.
439. Articoli sportivi. Sporting goods.
440. Ascensore. Elevator.
441. A (sinistra) destra. To the (left) right.
442. Attenzione! Look out; watch your step.
443. Attenzione al cane. Beware of the dog.
444. Automobili usate. Used cars.
445. Autonoleggio. Auto rentals.
446. Autorimessa. Garage.
447. Autoscuola. Driving school.
448. Autostrada. Highway.
449. Avanti. Come in.
450. Avviso pubblico. Public notice.
451. Avvocato. Lawyer.

452. Banca. Bank.
453. Bar. Coffee shop.
454. Barbiere. Barbershop.
455. Biancheria. Lingerie shop.
456. Biblioteca. Library.
457. Biciclette. Bicycles.
458. Biglietteria. Ticket office.
459. Biliardo. Billiards.
460. Birreria. Beer hall.
461. Bocce. Bowling.
462. Botteghino. Box office.
463. Buoni del Tesoro. Treasury Bonds.

464. Caffé. Bar; coffee shop.
465. Calcolatrici. Adding machines.
466. Caldo. Hot.
467. Calzoleria. Shoe store.
468. Cambio di programma. Change of program.
469. Cambio valute. Money exchanged.
470. Campeggio. Camping grounds.
471. Campidoglio. Capitol.
472. Camposanto. Cemetery.
473. Campo sportivo. Sports arena.
474. Carrozza ristorante. Dining car.
475. Cartoleria. Stationery store.
476. Casa di salute. Nursing home.

477. **Cassa di risparmio.** Savings bank.
478. **Cassetta postale.** Mailbox.
479. **Cavalcavia.** Overbridge.
480. **Chiamare.** Call.
481. **Chiuso dalle —— alle ——.** Closed from —— to ——.
482. **Chiuso i giorni festivi.** Closed on Sundays and holidays.
483. **Chiuso per ferie.** Closed for vacation.
484. **Cimitero.** Cemetery.
485. **Cinematografo.** Movies.
486. **Circolare.** Tram line that circles the town?
487. **Circolo sportivo.** Sports club.
488. **Città giardino.** Garden city.
489. **Compra-vendita terreni.** Real estate.
490. **Contravvenzione.** Fine.
491. **Cosmetici.** Cosmetics.
492. **Custode.** Caretaker.

493. **Dentista.** Dentist.
494. **Deposito.** Depot.
495. **Deposito bagagli.** Baggage checkroom.
496. **Deposito colli a mano.** Parcel checkroom.
497. **Direttissimo.** Express train.
498. **Discesa.** Descent.
499. **Diurno.** Public washrooms.
500. **Divieto di passaggio.** Crossing forbidden.

501. **Elenco telefonico.** Telephone directory.
502. **Entrata.** Entrance.
503. **Entrata libera.** Admission free.
504. **Entrata per gli addetti a lavoro.** Entrance for employees only.
505. **Esercito Italiano.** Italian army.
506. **Espresso.** Special delivery.

507. **Falegnameria.** Carpentry.
508. **Fermata autobus.** Bus stop.
509. **Fermata (obbligatoria) facoltativa.** Stop (on route) on signal.
510. **Fili ad alta tensione.** High-tension wires.
511. **Fiorista.** Flower shop.
512. **Fotografo.** Photographer.
513. **Freddo.** Cold.
514. **Frutta e verdura.** Fruits and vegetables.
515. **Fumatori.** Smoking allowed; smoking car.
516. **Funicolare.** Funicular railway.
517. **Funivia.** Cable railway.

518. **Gabinetti.**· Bathroom; toilet.
519. **Galleria.** Gallery (museum); tunnel.
520. **Galleria d'arte.** Art gallery.
521. **Gelati.** Ices; ice-cream.
522. **Gettone.** Token.
523. **Giardino botanico.** Botanical garden.
524. **Giardini pubblici.** Public gardens.
525. **Ginnasio.** Secondary school.

526. **Imbottiture e materassi.** Upholstery.
527. **Immondizie.** Garbage.
528. **Importazioni-Esportazioni.** Import and export.
529. **In alto.** Up.
530. **In basso.** Down.
531. **Ingresso (libero).** Admission (free).
532. **Insegne (luminose).** (Electric) signs.
533. **Inserire una moneta di (dieci lire).** Deposit (10 lire) coin.
534. **Interprete.** Interpreter.
535. **In vendita.** On sale here.
536. **Ipoteche.** Mortgages.
537. **Ippodromo.** Racecourse.
538. **Istituto commerciale.** Business school.

539. **Latteria.** Milk bar.
540. **Lavanderia e stiratoria.** Laundry.
541. **Lavori in corso.** Work going on.
542. **Libero.** Vacant.
543. **Libraio.** Bookseller.
544. **Libreria.** Bookshop.
545. **Liceo.** Higher secondary school.
546. **Lido.** Beach.
547. **Linee automobilistiche.** Bus lines.
548. **Linee tranviarie urbane.** Municipal tram lines.
549. **Locasi.** For rent.
550. **Lungomare.** Promenade along the shore line.

551. **Macchine da cucire.** Sewing machines.
552. **Macchine da scrivere.** Typewriters.
553. **Macelleria.** Butcher shop.
554. **Maglieria.** Knitted goods shop.
555. **Marina Italiana.** Italian navy.
556. **Mercato.** Market.
557. **Merceria.** Notions; haberdashery.
558. **Ministero.** Ministry.
559. **Mobilia.** Furniture.
560. **Modisteria.** Milliner.

561. Monte di pietà. Pawnshop.

562. Motociclette. Motorcycles.

563. Motoscafo. Motorboat (small).

564. Municipio. City hall.

565. Museo civico. City museum.

566. Museo nazionale. National museum.

567. Noleggio d'auto. Auto rentals.

568. Non fumatori. Non-smoker.

569. Non gettare commestibili agli animali.
Do not feed the animals.

570. Occasioni. Bargains.

571. Occupato. Engaged.

572. Oculista. Oculist.

573. Officina. Factory.

574. Officina riparazioni. Auto repairs.

575. Orario di visita. Visiting hours.

576. Orologeria. Watch shop.

577. Ortaggi. Vegetables.

578. Ospedale. Hospital.

579. Ospizio. Old people's home.

580. Ostello. Hostel.

581. Osteria. Inn.

582. Panetteria. Bakery shop.

583. Panificio. Bakery.

584. Parrucchiere. Men's hairdressing parlor.

585. Partenza. Departure.

586. Pedoni. Pedestrians.

587. Pericolo. Danger.

588. Pericolo (di fuoco) di morte. Danger (of fire) of death.

589. Pezzi di ricambio. Automobile parts.

590. Piccola pubblicità. Public notices.

591. Piscina comunale. City pool.

592. Pittura fresca. Wet paint.

593. Pitture e vernici. Paints.

594. Pizzicagnolo. Grocer.

595. Pizzicheria. Grocery.

596. Polizia stradale. Traffic police.

597. Pompe funebre. Funeral parlor.

598. Portinaio. Janitor.

599. Portineria. Janitor's quarters.

600. Poste e telegrafi. Post office.

601. Posteggio per auto pubbliche. Taxi stand.

602. Posto di ristoro. Buffet.

603. Posto riservato. Reserved seat.
604. Premere il bottone. Press button.
605. Prestiti su pegno. Loans.
606. Prezzi eccezionali. Bargains.
607. Procuratore. Attorney.
608. Proibito calpestare l'erba. Keep off the grass.
609. Proibito parlare al manovratore.
     Do not speak to the driver (conductor).
610. Pronto soccorso. First aid.
611. Proprietà privata. Private property.
612. Pubblicità. Advertisement.
613. Pulitura a secco. Dry cleaner.

614. Questura. Police station.
615. Quotazioni di borsa. Stock exchange report.

616. Rappresentazione sospesa. No performance.
617. Regali. Gifts.
618. Reggersi agli appositi sostegni. Hold on (in buses).
619. Ricordi. Gifts.
620. Ricovero. Shelter.
621. Rifiuti. Rubbish.
622. Rifornimento benzina. Filling station.
623. Rifugio. Shelter. (Also for mountain climbers.)
624. Rinfreschi. Refreshments.
625. Riparazioni. Repairs.
626. Ritrovo notturno. Night club.
627. Rivendita di legname. Lumber yard.
628. Rivolgersi allo sportello. Apply at window.
629. Rosticceria. Barbecue restaurant.

630. Sala d'aspetto. Waiting room.
631. Sala da ballo. Dance hall.
632. Sala da pranzo. Dining room.
633. Sala da tè. Tearoom.
634. Saldi. Inventory sale.
635. Sale e tabacchi. Tobacco shop.
636. Salire. Go up.
637. Salita. Ascent.
638. Salone di belleza. Beauty parlor.
639. Salumeria. Delicatessen.
640. Santuario. Shrine.
641. Sarta. Dressmaker.
642. Sarto. Tailor.
643. Sartoria. Couturier.
644. Sbarrato. Blocked. (Crossed.)

645. Scale. Stairs.
646. Scalo merci. Freight station.
647. Scampoli. Remnants.
648. Scarpe. Shoes.
649. Scendere. (Go) down.
650. Scuola di ballo. Dance studio.
651. Seggiovia. Chair lift.
652. Serale. Nightly.
653. Signore. Women; ladies.
654. Signori. Men; gentlemen.
655. Silenzio! Quiet please; no noise.
656. Si prega ——. You are requested to ——.
657. Sottopassaggio. Underpass.
658. Spegnere le luci. Turn off the lights.
659. Spettacolo continuo. Continuous performance.
660. Spingere. Push.
661. Stadio comunale. City stadium.
662. Stamperia. Printing.
663. Stazione ferroviaria. Railroad station.
664. Stazione marittima. Maritime station (dock).
665. Stoviglie. Pottery.
666. Sù. Up.
667. Suonare. Ring bell.

668. Tariffa ordinaria. Regular fee.
669. Tavola calda. Luncheonette.
670. Tavola riservata. Reserved table.
671. Telefono pubblico. Public telephone.
672. Televisione. Television.
673. Tipografia. Printing.
674. Tirare. Pull.
675. Tranvia a dentiera. Cog railway.
676. Trattoria. Restaurant.

677. Ufficio biglietti. Ticket office.
678. Ufficio informazioni. Information.
679. Ufficio prestiti. Loan office (in a bank).
680. Uomini. Men.
681. Uscita (di sicurezza). (Emergency) exit.

682. Vagone ristorante. Dining car.
683. Valute estere. Foreign exchange.
684. Vaporetto. Steamboat or yacht (for passengers).
685. Veleno. Per uso esterno. Poison. For external use only.
686. Vendesi. For sale.

687. Vendita al dettaglio. Retail.
688. Vendita all'ingrosso. Wholesale.
689. Vendita d'occasione. Bargain sale.
690. Vernice fresca. Wet paint.
691. Vestiario. Cloakroom.
692. Vietata l'affissione. Post no bills.
693. Vietato ai cani. No dogs allowed.
694. Vietato bagnarsi. No swimming; no bathing.
695. Vietato fumare. No smoking.
696. Vietato l'ingresso (ai non addetti al lavoro).
   No admittance (except on business).
697. Vietato sputare. No spitting.
698. Vietato transito biciclette. Cycling forbidden.
699. Vigili del fuoco. Firemen.
700. Vini e liquori. Wines and liquors.

COMMUNICATIONS: TELEPHONE

MEZZI DI COMUNICAZIONE: TELEFONO

701. May I make a telephone call?
   Mi permette di fare una telefonata?
   mee payr-MAYT-tay dee FAH-ray OO-nah tay-lay-fo-NAH-tah?

702. Will you telephone for me?
   Vorrebbe telefonare per me?
   vohr-REB-bay tay-lay-fo-NAH-ray payr may?

703. I want to make a local call.
   Vorrei fare una telefonata urbana.
   vohr-REH_ee FAH-ray OO-nah tay-lay-fo-NAH-tah oor-BAH-nah.

704. My number is ——.
   Il mio numero è ——.
   eel MEE-o NOO-may-ro eh ——

705. How much is a long-distance call to ——?
Quanto costa una telefonata interurbana per ——?
*KWAHN-toh KAW-stah OO-nah tay-lay-fo-NAH-tah
een-tayr-oor-BAH-nah payr ——?*

706. The operator will call you.
La centralinista vi chiama.
lah chayn-trah-lee-NEE-stah vee KYAH-mah.

707. Hello, hello.
Pronto.
PROHN-toh.

708. They do not answer.
Non risponde.
nawn ree-SPOHN-day.

709. It is busy.
È occupato.
eh ohk-koo-PAH-toh.

710. May I speak to the manager?
Potrei parlare al gerente?
po-TREH_ee pahr-LAH-ray ahl jayr-REN-tay?

711. This is Mr. —— speaking.
Parla il signor ——
PAHR-lah eel see-NYOHR ——.

712. Wait a moment, please.
Aspetti un momento, per favore.
ah-SPET-tee oon mo-MAYN-toh, payr fah-VO-ray.

713. He is not in.
Non c'è.
nawn cheh.

714. Will you make a note of this message?
Vuol prendere nota di questo messaggio?
*vwawl PREN-day-ray NAW-tah dee KWAY-sto
mays-SAHJ-jo?*

715. I will call back later.
Ritelefonerò più tardi.
ree-tay-lay-fo-nay-RAW pyoo TAHR-dee.

716. There is a telephone call for you.
È chiamato al telefono.
eh kyah-MAH-toh ahl tay-LEH-fo-no.

717. Good-bye.
Arrivederci.
ahr-ree-vay-DAYR-chee.

POST OFFICE
UFFICIO POSTALE

718. I am looking [for the post office].
Sto cercando [l'ufficio postale].
sto chayr-KAHN-doh [loof-FEE-chyoh po-STAH-lay].

719. —— a letter box.
una cassetta postale.
OO-nah kahs-SAYT-tah po-STAH-lay.

720. To which window should I go?
A quale sportello devo andare?
ah KWAH-lay spohr-TEL-lo DAY-vo ahn-DAH-ray?

721. I want to send this letter [via airmail].
Vorrei mandare questa lettera [per via aerea].
vohr-REH_ee mahn-DAH-ray KWAY-stah LET-tay-rah [payr VEE-ah ah_EH-ray-ah].

722. —— by regular (surface) mail.
per posta ordinaria.
payr PAW-stah ohr-dee-NAH-ryah.

723. —— **registered.**
raccomandata.
rahk-ko-mahn-DAH-tah.

724. —— **general delivery.**
fermo posta.
FAHR-mo PAW-stah.

725. —— **special delivery.**
per espresso.
payr ay-SPRES-so.

726. Can I send this [parcel post]?
Posso mandare questo [per pacco postale]?
*PAWS-so mahn-DAH-ray KWAY-sto [payr PAHK-ko
po-STAH-lay]?*

727. —— **air freight.**
per via aerea.
payr VEE-ah ah_EH-ray-ah.

728. I would like to insure this package for ——.
Vorrei assicurare questo pacco per ——.
*vohr-REH_ee ahs-see-koo-RAH-ray KWAY-sto
PAHK-ko payr ——.*

729. Please give me six thirty lire stamps.
Per favore mi dia sei (6) francobolli da trenta (30)
lire.
*payr fah-VO-ray mee DEE-ah SEH_ee frahn-ko-
BOHL-lee dah TRAYN-tah LEE-ray.*

730. Will it go out today?
Partirà oggi stesso?
pahr-tee-RAH AWJ-jee STAYS-so?

731. I want to send a money order.
Vorrei mandare un vaglia.
vor-REH_ee mahn-DAH-ray oon VAH-lyah.

TELEGRAM AND CABLEGRAM
TELEGRAMMA E CABLOGRAMMA

732. Please take [this cablegram].
Per favore spedisca [questo cablogramma].
payr fah-VO-ray spay-DEE-skah [KWAY-sto kah-blo-GRAHM-mah].

733. —— this telegram.
questo telegramma.
KWAY-sto tay-lay-GRAHM-mah.

734. —— this night letter.
questo telegramma-lettera.
KWAY-sto tay-lay-GRAHM-mah-LET-tay-rah.

735. What is the word rate to New York City?
Quant'è la tariffa per parola per New York?
kwahn-TEH lah tah-REEF-fah payr pah-RAW-lah payr New York?

736. Reply prepaid.
Risposta pagata.
ree-SPO-stah pah-GAH-tah.

737. When will it arrive?
Quando arriverà?
KWAHN-doh ahr-ree-vay-RAH?

HOTEL
ALL'ALBERGO

738. I am looking [for a good hotel].
Cerco [un buon albergo].
CHAYR-ko [oon bwawn ahl-BEHR-go].

739. —— the best hotel.
il migliore albergo.
eel mee-LYOH-ray ahl-BEHR-go.

740. —— **an inexpensive hotel.**

un albergo che non costi troppo.

oon ahl-BEHR-go kay nawn KAW-stee TRAWP-po.

741. —— **a boarding house.**

una pensione.

OO-nah payn-SYOH-nay.

742. I (do not) want to be in the center of town.

(Non) vorrei stare nel centro della città.

(nawn) vohr-REH_ee STAH-ray nayl CHEN-tro DAYL-lah cheet-TAH.

743. —— **where there is no noise.**

dove non c'è rumore.

DOH-vay nawn cheh roo-MO-ray.

744. I have a reservation for today.

Ho una prenotazione per oggi.

aw OO-nah pray-no-tah-TSYOH-nay payr AWJ-jee.

745. Do you have [a room]?

Ha [una camera]?

ah [OO-nah KAH-may-rah]?

746. —— **a single room.**

una camera a un letto.

OO-nah KAH-may-rah ah oon LET-toh.

747. —— **a double room.**

una camera a due letti.

OO-nah KAH-may-rah ah DOO-ay LET-tee.

748. —— **an air-conditioned room.**

una camera con aria condizionata.

OO-nah KAH-may-rah kohn AH-ryah kohn-dee-tsyoh-NAH-tah.

749. —— **a suite.**

un appartamento.

oon ahp-pahr-tah-MAYN-toh.

750. I want a room [with a double bed].
    Vorrei una camera [con letto matrimoniale].
    vohr-REH_ee OO-nah KAH-may-rah [kohn LET-toh
    mah-tree-mo-NYAH-lay].

751. —— with twin beds.
        a due letti.
        ah DOO-ay LET-tee.

752. —— with a bath.
        con bagno.
        kohn BAH-nyoh.

753. —— with a shower.
        con doccia.
        kohn DOHCH-chyah.

754. —— with running water.
        con acqua corrente.
        kohn AHK-kwah kohr-REN-tay.

755. —— with a balcony.
        con balcone.
        kohn bahl-KO-nay.

756. Is there a sink in the room?
    C'è il lavandino nella stanza?
    cheh eel lah-vahn-DEE-no NAYL-lah STAHN-tsah?

757. I will take a room [for tonight].
    Prendo una camera [per stanotte].
    PREN-doh OO-nah KAH-may-rah [payr stah-
    NAWT-tay].

758. —— for several days.
        per qualche giorno.
        payr KWAHL-kay JOHR-no.

759. —— for two persons.
        per due persone.
        payr DOO-ay payr-SO-nay.

760. May I have it [with] without meals?
La posso avere [con] senza i pasti?
lah PAWS-so ah-VAY-ray [kohn] SEN-tsah ee PAH-stee?

761. What is the rate per day?
Quanto costa al giorno?
KWAHN-toh KAW-stah ahl JOHR-no?

762. Are service and tax included?
Il servizio e le tasse sono inclusi?
eel sayr-VEE-tsyoh ay lay TAHS-say SO-no een-KLOO-zee?

763. I would like to see the room.
Vorrei vedere la camera.
vohr-REH_ee vay-DAY-ray lah KAH-may-rah.

764. I (do not) like this one.
Questa (non) mi piace.
KWAY-stah (nawn) mee PYAH-chay.

765. Have you something [better]?
Ha qualche cosa [di meglio]?
ah KWAHL-kay KAW-sah [dee MEH-lyoh]?

766. —— cheaper.
più a buon mercato.
pyoo ah bwawn mayr-KAH-toh.

767. —— larger.
più grande.
pyoo GRAHN-day.

768. —— smaller.
più piccolo.
pyoo PEEK-ko-lo.

769. An [outside] inside room.
Una stanza [esterna] interna.
OO-nah STAHN-tsah [ay-STEHR-nah] een-TEHR-nah.

770. On the first floor.
Al primo piano.
ahl PREE-mo PYAH-no.

771. On a [lower] higher floor.
Più in [basso] alto.
pyoo een [BAHS-so] AHL-toh.

772. With more [light] air.
Con più [luce] aria.
kohn pyoo [LOO-chay] AH-ryah.

773. [Upstairs] downstairs.
Al piano [superiore] inferiore.
ahl PYAH-no [soo-pay-RYOH-ray] een-fay-RYOH-ray.

774. Is there an elevator?
C'è l'ascensore?
cheh lah-shayn-SO-ray?

775. What is my room number?
Qual'è il numero della mia camera?
kwal-LEH eel NOO-may-ro DAYL-lah MEE-ah KAH-may-rah?

776. Please sign the hotel register.
Per favore firmi il registro.
payr fah-VO-ray FEER-mee eel ray-JEE-stro.

777. My room key, please.
La chiave della mia camera, per favore.
lah KYAH-vay DAYL-lah MEE-ah KAH-may-rah, payr fah-VO-ray.

778. Please send [the chambermaid].
Per favore, mandi [la cameriera].
payr fah-VO-ray, MAHN-dee [lah kah-may-RYEH-rah].

779. —— a bellhop.
il piccolo.
eel PEEK-ko-lo.

780. —— a porter.
un portabagagli.
oon pohr-tah-bah-GAH-lyee.

781. —— a valet.
un cameriere.
oon kah-may-RYEH-ray.

782. —— a messenger.
un fattorino.
oon faht-toh-REE-no.

783. Who is it?
Chi è?
kee eh?

784. Please [call me] wake me at 9 o'clock.
Per favore [mi chiami] mi svegli alle nove.
*payr fah-VO-ray [mee KYAH-mee] mee SVEH-lyee
AHL-lay NAW-vay.*

785. I would like to have breakfast in my room.
Vorrei fare colazione in camera.
*vohr-REH_ee FAH-ray ko-lah-TSYOH-nay een KAH-
may-rah.*

786. I want to speak to the manager.
Vorrei parlare col direttore.
vohr-REH_ee pahr-LAH-ray kohl dee-rayt-TOH-ray.

787. I wish to engage [a nurse] a baby sitter.
Vorrei assumere [un'infermiera] una ragazza per
guardare i bambini.
*vohr-REH_ee ahs-SOO-may-ray [oo-neen-fayr-MYEH-
rah] OO-nah rah-GAHT-tsah payr gwahr-DAH-ray
ee bahm-BEE-nee.*

788. Are there any letters or messages for me?
Ci sono lettere o messaggi per me?
chee SO-no LET-tay-ray o mays-SAHJ-jee payr may?

789. I am expecting [a visitor].
Aspetto [una visita].
ah-SPET-toh [OO-nah VEE-zee-tah].

790. —— a telephone call.
una telefonata.
OO-nah tay-lay-fo-NAH-tah.

791. —— a package.
un pacco.
oon PAHK-ko.

792. At what time must I check out of the room?
A che ora bisogna disdire la camera?
ah kay O-rah bee-ZO-nyah dee-ZDEE-ray lah KAH-may-rah?

793. Make out my bill now because I am leaving immediately.
Mi prepari il conto adesso perchè parto subito.
mee pray-PAH-ree eel KOHN-toh ah-DES-so payr-KAY PAHR-toh SOO-bee-toh.

794. Will you accept my personal check?
Accetta un mio assegno personale?
ahch-CHET-tah oon MEE-o ahs-SAY-nyoh payr-so-NAH-lay?

795. Forward my mail to American Express in Paris.
Faccia proseguire la mia corrispondenza all'American Express a Parigi.
FAHCH-chyah pro-say-GWEE-ray lah MEE-ah kohr-ree-spohn-DEN-tsah ahl-lAmerican Express ah pah-REE-jee.

CHAMBERMAID

LA CAMERIERA

796. Do not disturb me until 7 o'clock.
Non mi disturbi prima delle sette.
nawn mee dee-STOOR-bee PREE-mah DAYL-lay SET-tay.

797. [The door] the lock does not work well.
[La porta] la serratura non funziona bene.
[lah PAWR-tah] lah sayr-rah-TOO-rah nawn foon-TSYOH-nah BEH-nay.

798. The room is too [cold] hot.
La stanza è troppo [fredda] calda.
lah STAHN-tsah eh TRAWP-po [FRAYD-dah] KAHL-dah.

799. Could I have some things washed?
Posso far lavare qualche cosa?
PAWS-so fahr lah-VAH-ray KWAHL-kay KAW-sah?

800. Please bring me [another blanket].
Per favore mi porti [un'altra coperta].
payr fah-VO-ray mee PAWR-tee [oo-nahl-trah ko-PEHR-tah].

801. —— a bath mat.
uno stoino per bagno.
OO-no sto-EE-no payr BAH-nyoh.

802. —— some coat hangers.
degli attaccapanni.
DAY-lyee aht-tahk-kahp-PAHN-nee.

803. —— a glass.
un bicchiere.
oon beek-KYEH-ray.

804. —— **a pillow.**
un cuscino.
oon koo-SHEE-no.

805. —— **a pillowcase.**
una federa.
OO-nah FEH-day-rah.

806. —— **some soap.**
del sapone.
dayl sah-PO-nay.

807. —— **some toilet tissue.**
della carta igienica.
DAYL-lah KAHR-tah ee-JYEH-nee-kah.

808. —— **some towels.**
degli asciugamani.
DAY-lyee ah-shyoo-gah-MAH-nee.

809. —— **some washcloths.**
degli asciugamanini.
DAY-lyee ah-shyoo-gah-mah-NEE-nee.

810. —— **some sponges.**
delle spugne.
DAY-lyee SPOO-nyay.

811. —— **some drinking water.**
dell'acqua da bere.
dayl-LAHK-kwah dah BAY-ray.

812. Change the sheets.
Cambi le lenzuola.
KAHM-bee lay layn-TSWAW-lah.

813. Make up the bed for me.
Mi rifaccia il letto.
mee ree-FAHCH-chyah eel LET-toh.

814. Please come back later.
Per favore ritorni più tardi.
payr fah-VO-ray ree-TOHR-nee pyoo TAHR-dee.

APARTMENT
L'APPARTAMENTO

815. I am looking for a furnished apartment [with a bathroom].
Cerco un appartamento ammobiliato [con stanza da bagno].
CHAYR-ko oon ahp-pahr-tah-MAYN-toh ahm-mo-bee-LYAH-toh [kohn STAHN-tsah dah BAH-nyoh].

816. —— with two bedrooms.
con due camere da letto.
kohn DOO-ay KAH-may-ray dah LET-toh.

817. —— with a dining room.
con sala da pranzo.
kohn SAH-lah dah PRAHN-dzo.

818. —— with a kitchen.
con cucina.
kohn koo-CHEE-nah.

819. —— with a living room.
con salotto.
kohn sah-LAWT-toh.

820. Do you furnish [the linen]?
Fornisce anche [la biancheria da letto]?
fohr-NEE-shay AHN-kay [lah byahn-kay-REE-ah dah LET-toh]?

821. —— the dishes.
i piatti.
ee PYAHT-tee.

822. —— the silverware.
le posate.
lay po-SAH-tay.

823. —— the cooking utensils.
gli utensili da cucina.
lyee oo-tayn-SEE-lee dah koo-CHEE-nah.

824. Do you know [a good cook] a housemaid?
Conosce [una buona cuoca] una donna di servizio?
ko-NO-shay [OO-nah BWAW-nah KWAW-ka] OO-nah DAWN-nah dee sayr-VEE-tsyoh?

RESTAURANT

AL RISTORANTE

825. Can you recommend a (native) restaurant?
Mi potrebbe raccomandare un ristorante (di specialità del luogo)?
mee po-TREB-bay rahk-ko-mahn-DAH-ray oon reesto-RAHN-tay (dee spay-chyah-lee-TAH dayl LWAW-go)?

826. —— for breakfast.
per la prima colazione.
payr lah PREE-mah ko-lah-TSYOH-nay.

827. —— for lunch.
per la colazione.
payr lah ko-lah-TSYOH-nay.

828. —— for supper.
per la cena.
payr lah CHAY-nah.

829. Where can I buy a sandwich?
Dove potrei comprare un panino imbottito?
DOH-vay po-TREH_ee kohm-PRAH-ray oon pah-NEE-no eem-boht-TEE-toh?

830. At what time is dinner served?
A che ora si va a pranzo?
ah kay O-rah see vah ah PRAHN-dzo?

831. Can we [lunch] dine now?
Si può [fare colazione] pranzare ora?
see pwaw [FAH-ray ko-lah-TSYOH-nay] prahn-DZAH-ray O-rah?

832. Are you [my waiter]?
Lei è [il mio cameriere]?
LEH-_ee eh [eel MEE-o kah-may-RYEH-ray]?

833. —— my waitress.
la mia cameriera.
lah MEE-ah kah-may-RYEH-rah.

834. —— the headwaiter.
il capocameriere.
eel kah-po-kah-may-RYEH-ray.

835. Waiter!
Cameriere!
kah-may-RYEH-ray!

836. Give us a table [near the window].
Ci dia una tavola [vicino alla finestra].
chee DEE-ah OO-nah TAH-vo-lah [vee-CHEE-no AHL-lah fee-NEH-strah].

837. —— outside.
fuori.
FWAW-ree.

838. —— inside.
dentro.
DAYN-tro.

839. —— **at the side.**
    da una parte.
    dah OO-nah PAHR-tay.

840. —— **in the corner.**
    nell'angolo.
    nayl-LAHN-go-lo.

841. —— **for four persons.**
    per quattro persone.
    payr KWAHT-tro payr-SO-nay.

842. Please serve us quickly.
    Per favore ci serva subito.
    payr fah-VO-ray chee SEHR-vah SOO-bee-toh.

843. We want to dine [à la carte].
    Vogliamo mangiare [alla carta].
    vo-LYAH-mo mahn-JAH-ray [AHL-lah KAHR-tah].

844. —— **table d'hôte.**
    a prezzo fisso.
    ah PRET-tso FEES-so.

845. What is the specialty of this restaurant?
    Qual'è la specialità di questo ristorante?
    kwah-LEH lah spay-chyah-lee-TAH dee KWAY-sto ree-sto-RAHN-tay?

846. Please bring me [the menu].
    Per favore mi porti [la lista].
    payr fah-VO-ray mee PAWR-tee [lah LEE-stah].

847. —— **the wine list.**
    la lista dei vini.
    lah LEE-stah day VEE-nee.

848. —— **some bread and butter.**
    del pane e burro.
    dayl PAH-nay ay BOOR-ro.

849. —— bread sticks.
dei grissini.
day grees-SEE-nee.

850. —— drinking water.
dell'acqua da bere.
dayl-LAHK-kwah dah BAY-ray.

851. —— water [with] without ice.
dell'acqua [con] senza ghiaccio.
dayl-LAHK-kwah [kohn] SEN-tsah GYAHCH-
chyoh.

852. —— a fork.
una forchetta.
OO-nah fohr-KAYT-tah.

853. —— a knife.
un coltello.
oon kohl-TEL-lo.

854. —— a teaspoon.
un cucchiaino.
oon kook-kyah-EE-no.

855. —— a large spoon.
un cucchiaio.
oon kook-KYAH-yo.

856. —— a napkin.
un tovagliolo.
oon toh-vah-LYAW-lo.

857. —— a plate.
un piatto.
oon PYAHT-toh.

858. I would like something [simple].
Mi piacerebbe qualche cosa [semplice].
mee pyach-chayr-REB-bay KWAHL-kay KAW-sah
[SAYM-plee-chay].

859. —— **not too spicy.**
   non troppo piccante.
   nawn TRAWP-po peek-KAHN-tay.

860. —— **not too sweet.**
   non troppo dolce.
   nawn TRAWP-po DOHL-chay.

861. —— **not too sour.**
   non troppo acido.
   nawn TRAWP-po AH-chee-doh.

862. —— **not too fat.**
   non troppo grasso.
   nawn TRAWP-po GRAHS-so.

863. —— **not too tough.**
   non troppo duro.
   nawn TRAWP-po DOO-roh.

864. A little [more] less, please.
   Un po' [di più] meno, per favore.
   oon paw [dee pyoo] MAY-no, payr fah-VO-ray.

865. I have had [enough] too much of it.
   Ne ho avuto [abbastanza] troppo.
   *nay   aw   ah-VOO-toh   [ahb-bah-STAHN-tsah]
      TRAWP-po.*

866. I like the meat cooked [rare].
   Mi piace la carne [al sangue].
   mee PYAH-chay lah KAHR-nay [ahl SAHN-gway].

867. —— **medium.**
   non troppo cotta.
   nawn TRAWP-po KAWT-tah.

868. —— **well done.**
   ben cotta.
   ben KAWT-tah.

869. It is [overcooked] undercooked.
È [troppo cotto] troppo poco cotto.
*eh [TRAWP-po KAWT-toh] TRAWP-po PAW-ko
KAWT-toh.*

870. This is cold.
Questo è freddo.
KWAY-sto eh FRAYD-doh.

871. Take it away, please.
Lo porti via, per favore.
lo PAWR-tee VEE-ah, payr fah-VO-ray.

872. I did not order this.
Non ho ordinato questo.
nawn aw ohr-dee-NAH-toh KWAY-sto.

873. May I change this for a salad?
Posso cambiare questo con un'insalata?
*PAWS-so kahm-BYAH-ray KWAY-sto kohn oo-neen-
sah-LAH-tah?*

874. The check, please.
Il conto, per favore.
eel KOHN-toh, payr fah-VO-ray.

875. Are the tip and service charge included?
La mancia e il servizio sono inclusi?
*lah MAHN-chyah ay eel sayr-VEE-tsyoh SO-no
een-KLOO-zee?*

876. I think there is a mistake in the bill.
Credo che ci sia uno sbaglio nel conto.
*CRAY-doh kay chee SEE-ah OO-no SBAH-lyoh nayl
KOHN-toh.*

877. What is this for?
Questo per che cos'è?
KWAY-sto payr kay kaw-SEH?

878. The food and service were excellent.
Il cibo e il servizio sono stati eccellenti.
eel CHEE-bo ay eel sayr-VEE-tsyoh SO-no STAH-tee aych-chayl-LEN-tee.

879. Keep the change.
Tenga il resto.
TEN-gah eel REH-sto.

880. Hearty appetite!
Buon appetito!
bwawn ahp-pay-TEE-toh!

CAFÉ: DRINKS and WINES
AL CAFFÈ: BEVANDE e VINI

881. Bartender, I'd like to have something to drink.
Barista, vorrei qualche cosa da bere.
bah-REE-stah vohr-REH_ee KWAHL-kay KAW-sah dah BAY-ray.

882. To your health!
Alla salute!
AHL-lah sah-LOO-tay.

883. Let's have another.
Prendiamone un altro.
pren-DYAH-mo-nay oon AHL-tro.

884.* Anisetta. *ah-nee-ZET-tah.* A liqueur made with the aromatic herb, anise.

885. Aperitivo. *ah-payr-ree-TEE-vo.* A wine drink usually taken before dinner.

885a. Bardolino. *bahr-doh-LEE-no.* Dry red wine from Garda Lake.

---

* This list has been alphabetized in Italian to facilitate the tourists' reading of Italian wine lists.

886. Birra.   *BEER-rah.*   Beer.

887. Chianti.   *KYAHN-tee.*   Dry red wine from Tuscany.

888. Cinque terre.   *CHEEN-kway TEHR-ray.*   Sweet white wine.

889. Cognac.   *KO-nyahk.*   Cognac.

890. Cordiale.   *kohr-DYAHL-lay.*   Cordial.

891. Frascati.   *frah-SKAH-tee.*   Dry, white, medium-sweet wine from the vicinity of Rome.

892. Gassosa.   *gahs-SO-sah.*   Soda water.

893. Grappa.   *GRAHP-pah.*   A cheap brandy.

894. Lacrima Christi.   *lah-KREE-mah KREE-stee.*   Dry red wine.

895. Liquore.   *lee-KWAW-ray.*   Liqueur.

896. Marsala.   *mahr-SAH-lah.*   Sweet, dry, amber-colored wine from Sicily.

897. Moscato.   *mo-SKAH-toh.*   Semi-sweet dessert wine.

898. Orvieto.   *ohr-VYAY-toh.*   Sweet, dry, white wine from Orvieto.

899. Orzata.   *ohr-DZAH-tah.*   Soft drink made of barley water.

900. Sidro.   *SEE-dro.*   Cider.

901. Soave bianco.   *so-AH-vay BYAHN-ko.*   Dry, white wine.

902. Spumante.   *spoo-MAHN-tay.*   Sparkling, bubbling wine.

903. Strega.   *STRAY-gah.*   Liqueur made from fermented plums.

904. Valpolicella.   *vahl-po-lee-CHEL-lah.*   Dry, red wine.

905. Vermouth. *VAYR-moot.* Dry, white or sweet, red wine served as an apéritif.

906. Whiskey e soda. "*whiskey*" *ay SAW-dah.* Whiskey and soda.

907. Vino. *VEE-no.* Wine.

BREAKFAST FOODS*
PER LA PRIMA COLAZIONE

908. Cereale cotto. *chay-ray-AH-lay KAWT-toh.* Cooked cereal.

909. Frittata. *freet-TAH-tah.* Omelet.

910. Pancetta. *pahn-CHAYT-tah.* A kind of bacon.

911. Pane tostato e marmellata. *PAH-nay toh-STAH-toh ay mahr-mayl-LAH-tah.* Toast and jam.

912. Panini. *pah-NEE-nee.* Rolls.

913. Prugne cotte. *PROO-nyay KAWT-tay.* Stewed prunes.

914. Succo d'arancio. *SOOK-ko dah-RAHN-chyoh.* Orange juice.

915. Succo di frutta. *SOOK-ko dee FROOT-tah.* Fruit juice.

916. Succo di pomodoro. *SOOK-ko dee po-mo-DAW-ro.* Tomato juice.

917. Uova à la coque. *WAW-vah ah lah KOH-kway.* Soft-boiled eggs.

* All food lists are alphabetized in Italian to facilitate the reading of Italian menus.

918. Uova al prosciutto. *WAW-vah ahl pro-wa.
SHYOOT-toh.* Ham and eggs.

919. Uova bazzotte. *WAW-vah bahd-DZAWT-tay.*
Four-minute eggs.

920. Uova con bacon. *WAW-vah kohn "bacon."*
Bacon and eggs.

921. Uova fritte. *WAW-vah FREET-tay.* Fried
eggs.

922. Uova sode. *WAW-vah SAW-day.* Hard-boiled
eggs.

923. Uova strapazzate. *WAW-vah strah-paht-TSAH-
tay.* Scrambled eggs.

SOUPS AND APPETIZERS

MINESTRE IN BRODO E ANTI-PASTI*

924. Antipasto variato. *ahn-tee-PAH-sto vah-RYAH-
toh.* Assorted hors d'œuvres.

925. Brodo di pollo. *BRAW-doh dee POHL-lo.*
Chicken soup.

926. Cacciucco. *kah-CHYOOK-koh.* Soup made of
fish and shell fish and highly seasoned.

927. Crostini di fegato di pollo. *kro-STEE-nee dee
FAY-gah-toh dee POHL-lo.* Chicken liver appe-
tizers.

928. Insalata russa. *een-sah-LAH-tah ROOS-sah.*
Salad mold of vegetables and egg.

929. Melone e prosciutto. *may-LO-nay ay pro-
SHYOOT-toh.* Melon with ham.

* Antipasto is served as a simple or elaborate dish. Ingredients
are always varied and tend to consist of the local food products.

930. Minestra di verdure. *mee-NEH-strah dee vehr-DOO-ray.* Vegetable soup.

931. Minestrone. *meen-ay-STROH-nay.* Vegetable soup with pasta or rice.

932. Minestrone alla genovese. *mee-nay-STRO-nay AHL-lah jay-no-VAY-say.* Minestrone flavored with pesto (a Genoese sauce of basil, pecorino cheese, garlic and pine nuts soaked in oil).

933. Pasta e fagioli. *PAH-stah ay fah-JAW-lee.* Soup made with beans, macaroni and pork rind.

934. Pasta reale. *PAH-stah ray-AH-lay.* Small balls of flaky dough used in soups.

935. Prosciutto. *pro-SHYOOT-toh.* Ham (dried, spiced but not smoked).

936. Risi e bisi. *REE-see ay BEE-see.* Rice soup with peas, onions, bacon and ham.

937. Stracciatella. *strahch-chyah-TEL-lah.* Egg soup.

938. Zuppa alla pavese. *TSOOP-pah AHL-lah pah-VAY-say.* Soup poured over poached eggs.

939. Zuppa di pesce. *TSOOP-pah dee PAY-shay.* Thick fish soup.

STYLES OF PREPARATION

The following expressions are frequently seen on American and Italian menus. They refer to the particular style of preparation and are not reserved for any specific dish.

940. Affumicato. *ah-foo-me-KAH-toh.* Smoked.

941. Ai ferri. *AH_ee FEHR-ree.* On the spit.

942. Al burro. *ahl BOOR-roh.* With butter.

943. Al dente. *ahl DEN-tay.* Cooked until just ready—to describe spaghetti.

944. Al forno. *ahl FOHR-no.* Baked.

945. Alla griglia. *AHL-lah GREE-lyah.* Grilled.

946. Alla marinara. *AHL-lah mah-ree-NAH-rah.* Cooked in tomato sauce and seasoned with garlic, oil and parsley.

947. Alle acciughe. *AHL-lay ahch-CHYOO-gay.* Prepared with anchovies.

948. Alle vongole. *AHL-lay VOHN-go-lay.* Prepared with clams.

949. All'olio ed aglio. *ahl-LAW-lyoh ed AHL-lyoh.* With oil and garlic.

950. All'uovo. *ahl-LWAW-vo.* With eggs.

951. Al pomodoro. *ahl po-mo-DAW-ro.* With tomato sauce.

952. Al ragù. *ahl rah-GOO.* With meat sauce.

953. Al sugo. *ahl SOO-go.* With meat sauce.

954. Arreganato. *ahr-ray-gah-NAH-toh.* Prepared with oregano.

955. Brodetto. *bro-DAY-toh.* Served in rich, thick gravy.

956. Fra Diavolo. *frah DYAH-vo-lo.* Prepared with a spicy tomato sauce.

957. Fritto. *free-toh.* Fried.

958. Incanestrato. *een-kah-nes-TRAH-toh.* In the basket.

959. In padella. *een pah-DEL-lah.* Fried.

960. Pizzaiola. *peet-tsah-YAW-lah.* Pizza style (with mozzarella cheese and tomato sauce).

MACARONI AND RICE DISHES

MINESTRE ASCIUTTE: PASTA

961. Arancini.   *ah-rahn-CHEE-nee.*   Little balls of rice mixed with liver, meat, mushrooms, onions, spices; breaded and fried in olive oil.

962. Cannelloni.   *kahn-nayl-LO-nee.*   Large, round envelopes of flaky pastry dough stuffed with minced meat or fish.

963. Fettuccine alla papalina.   *fayt-tooch-CHEE-nay AHL-lah pah-pah-LEE-nah.*   Thin egg noodles flavored with ham and butter.

964. Fettuccine alla romana.   *fayt-tooch-CHEE-nay AHL-lah ro-MAH-nah.*   Thin egg noodles and beef stew.

965. Fettuccine all'uovo.   *fayt-tooch-CHEE-nay ahl-LAW-vo.*   Thin egg noodles with meat sauce.

966. Gnocchi.   *NYAWK-kee.*   Dumplings made of potatoes and flour or of semolina, cooked in water and served with sauce and Parmesan cheese.

967. Lasagne.   *lah-ZAH-nyay.*   Very wide egg noodles prepared with meat sauce, ricotta, mozzarella and baked.

968. Maccheroni alla marinara.   *mahk-kay-RO-nee AHL-lah mah-ree-NAH-rah.*   Macaroni prepared with garlic, oil and parsley.

969. Manicotti.   *mah-nee-KAWT-tee.*   Large tubes of macaroni stuffed with cheese, meat and baked in a sauce.

970. Pappardelle.   *pahp-pahr-DEL-lay.*   Lasagne prepared in a game sauce with hare or duck.

971. Pasta asciutta. *PAH-stah ah-SHYOOT-tah.* Macaroni flavored with sauce.

972. Pasticciata. *pah-steech-CHYAH-tah.* Strips of egg dough, seasoned with meat sauce, mozzarella, flour paste or cream and baked.

973. Pasticcio di maccheroni. *pah-STEECH-chyoh dee mahk-kay-RO-nee.* Macaroni and cheese casserole.

974. Pizza. *PEET-tsah.* Round, flat dough baked with cheese, seasonings, tomato sauce, anchovies or sausage.

975. Polenta. *po-LEN-tah.* Yellow cornmeal mush.

976. Polenta e osei. *po-LEN-tah ay o-SEH_ee.* Yellow cornmeal mush garnished with small roasted birds and gravy.

977. Ravioli. *rah-VYAW-lee.* Small pockets of dough stuffed with meat or vegetables, boiled and served with sauce.

978. Rigatoni. *ree-gah-TOH-nee.* Large macaroni with grooves.

979. Risotto. *ree-SAWT-toh.* Boiled rice with sauce.

980. Risotto alla milanese. *ree-SAWT-toh AHL-lah mee-lah-NAY-say.* Boiled rice with chicken livers and minced meat balls, seasoned with saffron.

981. Spaghetti alla carrettiera. *spah-GAYT-tee AHL-lah kahr-rayt-TYEH-rah.* Spaghetti with a sauce made of tuna fish, mushrooms and tomatoes.

982. Spaghetti alla carbonàra. *spah-GAYT-tee AHL-lah kahr-bo-NAH-rah.* Spaghetti with a sauce made of bacon, cheese and eggs.

983. Spaghetti alla matriciana. *spah-GAYT-tee ahl-lah mah-tree-CHYAH-nah.* Spaghetti with a sauce made of pork and tomatoes and topped with pecorino cheese.

984. Spiedini. *spyay-DEE-nee.* Sliced Italian bread spread with mozzarella, anchovies and then fried.

985. Tagliatelle. *tah-lyah-TEL-lay.* Home made egg noodles.

986. Tagliatelle al ragù. *tah-lyah-TEL-lay ahl rah-GOO.* Noodles with meat sauce.

987. Tagliatelle verdi. *tah-lyah-TEL-lay VAYR-dee.* Green egg noodles, made by mixing the dough with spinach.

988. Torta pasqualina. *TOHR-tah pah-skwah-LEE-nah.* Paper-thin layers of dough with a stuffing of green vegetables, cottage cheese and eggs.

989. Tortellini. *tohr-tayl-LEE-nee.* Small pockets of dough filled with minced pork, turkey, ham, eggs, cheese and spices and served in broth or meat sauce. (A specialty of Bologna.)

POULTRY, MEAT AND GAME
POLLI, CARNE E SELVAGGINA

990. Abbacchio. *ahb-BAHK-kyoh.* Young spring lamb.

991. Abbacchio al forno. *ahb-BAHK-kyoh ahl FOHR-no.* Oven baked spring lamb. (A Roman specialty.)

992. Agnello. *ah-NYEL-lo.* Lamb.

993. Animelle.   *ah-nee-MEL-lay.*   Sweetbreads.

994. Anitra arrosto.   *AH-nee-trah   ahr-RAW-sto.*
Roast duck.

995. Arista.   *ah-REE-stah.*   Loin of pork roasted in
the oven or on the spit.

996. Arrosto di agnello con patatine.   *ahr-RAW-
sto dee ah-NYEL-lo kohn pah-tah-TEE-nay.*   Roast
spring lamb with new potatoes.

997. Bistecca.   *bee-STEK-kah.*   Steak.

998. Bistecca alla Fiorentina.   *bee-STAYK-kah
AHL-lah   fyoh-rayn-TEE-nah.*   Porterhouse
steak, charcoal broiled and served with lemon
wedges.

999. Bistecca di maiale.   *bee-STAYK-kah dee mah-
YAH-lay.*   Pork chops.

1000. Braciola di manzo.   *brah-CHYAW-lah   dee
MAHN-dzo.*   Beef cutlet.

1001. Busecca.   *boo-ZEK-kah.*   Highly spiced veal
tripe with beans.

1002. Cappone magro.   *kahp-PO-nay   MAH-gro.*
Lean capon.

1003. Cervello.   *chayr-VEL-lo.*   Scrambled calf or
pork brains.

1004. Cima di vitello.   *CHEE-mah dee vee-TEL-lo.*
Jellied veal.

1005. Coniglio.   *ko-NEE-lyoh.*   Rabbit.

1006. Costolette di maiale.   *ko-sto-LET-tay dee mah-
YAH-lay.*   Pork chops.

1007. Cotechino.   *ko-tay-KEE-no.*   Highly spiced
pork sausage.

1008. Cotoletta alla milanese. *ko-toh-LAYT-tah AHL-lah mee-lah-NAY-say.* Veal cutlet, breaded and fried.

1009. Fagiano. *fah-JAH-no.* Pheasant.

1010. Fegato. *FAY-gah-toh.* Liver.

1011. Fegato alla veneziana. *FAY-gah-toh AHL-lah vay-nay-TSYAH-nah.* Strips of liver sautéed with onions and bacon.

1012. Filetto di bue. *fee-LET-toh dee BOO-ay.* Filet of beef.

1013. Filetto di manzo. *fee-LAYT-toh dee MAHN-dzo.* Thin beef steak.

1014. Fritto misto. *FREET-toh MEE-sto.* Mixed grill of liver, heart, brains, steak, cocks-comb, etc.

1015. Involtini. *een-vohl-TEE-nee.* Sliced meat rolled around ham, sage and Parmesan cheese. Stewed in broth and served in sauce.

1016. Lepre. *LEH-pray.* Hare.

1017. Lingua. *LEEN-gwah.* Tongue.

1018. Maiale. *mah-YAH-lay.* Pork.

1019. Manzo arrosto. *MAHN-dzo ahr-RAW-sto.* Roast beef.

1020. Misto alla griglia. *MEE-sto AHL-lah GREE-lyah.* Mixed grill.

1021. Mortadella. *mohrt-tah-DEL-lah.* A kind of bologna.

1022. Oca. *AW-kah.* Goose.

1023. Olivetto di vitello. *oh-lee-VAYT-tay dee vee-TEL-lo.* Folded slices of veal cooked with white wine and spices.

1024. Ossobuco milanese.   *ohs-so-BOO-ko mee-lah-NAY-say*.   Veal knuckle with rice.

1025. Porchetta.   *pohr-KAYT-tah*.   Whole suckling pig, salted, spiced and prepared in the oven.

1026. Pernice.   *payr-NEE-chay*.   Partridge.

1027. Piccioncini con risotto.   *peech-chyohn-CHEE-nee kohn ree-SAWT-toh*.   Squabs prepared on the spit and served with rice.

1028. Pollo ai ferri.   *POHL-lo AH_ee FEHR-ree*.   Broiled chicken.

1029. Pollo fritto.   *POHL-lo FREET-toh*.   Fried chicken.

1030. Polpette.   *pohl-PAYT-tay*.   Meat balls.

1031. Polpettone.   *pohl-payt-TOH-nay*.   Meat loaf.

1032. Rognone.   *ro-NYOH-nay*.   Kidney.

1033. Salame.   *sah-LAH-may*.   Spiced pork.

1034. Salsicce.   *sahl-SEECH-chay*.   Highly spiced pork sausage.

1035. Saltimbocca alla romana.   *sahl-teem-BOHK-kah AHL-lah ro-MAH-nah*.   Veal prepared with sage and ham, sautéed in butter and sprinkled with Marsala wine.

1036. Sanguinaccio.   *sahn-gwee-NAH-chyoh*.   Blood sausage.

1037. Scallopine.   *skah-lohp-PEE-nay*.   Veal cutlets.

1038. Scaloppine ai funghi.   *skah-lohp-PEE-nay AH_ee FOON-gee*.   Veal cutlets with mushrooms.

1039. Spezzatino di vitello.   *spayt-tsah-TEE-no dee vee-TEL-lo*.   Veal stew.

1040. **Stufato di manzo.** *stoo-FAH-toh dee MAHN-dzo.* Beef stew.

1041. **Supplì al telefono.** *soop-PLEE ahl tay-LEH-fo-no.* Elongated shapes of rice filled with giblets, mozzarella or mushrooms and tomato sauce.

1042. **Tacchino ripieno.** *tahk-KEE-no ree-PYEH-no.* Stuffed turkey.

1043. **Trippa al sugo.** *TREEP-pah ahl SOO-go.* Tripe with meat sauce.

1044. **Uccelletti.** *oo-chayl-LAYT-tee.* Strips of veal, rolled and stuffed.

1045. **Vitello.** *vee-TEL-lo.* Veal.

1046. **Zampone.** *tsahm-PO-nay.* Highly seasoned pork made up into sausages in the skin of the pig's forefeet.

FISH AND SEA FOOD
PESCI E FRUTTI DI MARE

1047. **Acciughe.** *ahch-CHYOO-gay.* Anchovies.

1048. **Alici.** *ah-LEE-chee.* Anchovies preserved in olive oil.

1049. **Anguille alla veneziana.** *ahn-GWEEL-lay AHL-lah vay-nay-TSYAH-nah.* Eels cooked in tunny and lemon sauce.

1050. **Aragosta.** *ah-rah-GO-stah.* Lobster.

1051. **Aragosta alla termidoro.** *ah-rah-GO-stah AHL-lah tayr-mee-DAW-ro.* Lobster Thermidor.

1052. Aringa. *ah-REEN-gah.* Herring.

1053. Baccalà alla marinara. *bahk-kah-LAH AHL-lah mah-ree-NAH-rah.* Dried cod fish, sailor style.

1054. Brodetto di pesce alla veneziana. *bro-DAYT-toh dee PAY-shay AHL-lah vay-nay-TSYAH-nah.* Fish stew with thick gravy and saffron.

1055. Cacciucco. *kah-CHYOOK-ko.* Fish stew.

1056. Calamari. *kah-lah-MAH-ree.* Cuttlefish.

1057. Caviale. *kah-VYAH-lay.* Caviar.

1058. Cozza. *KAW-tsah.* Mussel.

1059. Fritto misto mare. *FREET-toh MEE-sto MAH-ray.* Grill of sea foods.

1060. Gamberi. *GAHM-bay-ree.* Crabs.

1061. Lumache. *loo-MAH-kay.* Snails.

1062. Merluzzo. *mayr-LOOT-tso.* Fresh cod.

1063. Ostriche. *AW-stree-kay.* Clams.

1064. Pesciolino. *pays-shyaw-LEE-no.* Whitebait.

1065. Polpi. *POHL-pee.* Squid.

1066. Riccio. *REE-chyoh.* Sea urchin.

1067. Salmon. *sahl-MO-nay.* Salmon.

1068. Sardine. *sahr-DEE-nay.* Sardines.

1069. Scampi. *SKAHM-pee.* A variety of shrimp prepared in many different styles; also served in soups and sauces.

1070. Scungilli. *skoon-JEEL-lee.* Conch meat extracted from the shell, boiled and served with a hot sauce.

1071. **Seppie al pomodoro.** *SAYP-pyay ahl po-mo-DAW-ro.* Cuttlefish in tomato sauce.

1072. **Sogliola.** *SAW-lyoh-lah.* Sole.

1073. **Stoccafisso accomodato.** *stohk-kah-FEES-so ahk-ko-mo-DAH-toh.* Dried cod prepared with milk, oil, anchovies, chopped walnuts and black olives.

1074. **Tonno.** *TOHN-no.* Tuna fish.

1075. **Trota.** *TRAW-tah.* Trout.

1076. **Triglie alla livornese.** *TREE-lyay AHL-lah lee-vohr-NAY-say.* Mullet seasoned with chopped garlic, parsley and celery; cooked in oil with pepper and slices of tomato.

1077. **Vongole.** *VOHN-go-lay.* Very small, tasty clams.

VEGETABLES AND SALAD

VERDURE E INSALATE

1078. **Asparagi.** *ah-SPAH-rah-jee.* Asparagus.

1079. **Barbabietole.** *bahr-bah-BYEH-toh-lay.* Beets.

1080. **Broccoli.** *BRAWK-ko-lee.* Broccoli.

1081. **Caponatina.** *kah-paw-nah-TEE-nah.* Pickled vegetables.

1082. **Capperi.** *KAHP-pay-ree.* Capers.

1083. **Carciofi.** *kahr-CHYAW-fee.* Artichokes.

1084. **Carciofini.** *kahr-chyoh-FEE-nee.* Artichoke hearts in olive oil.

1085. **Cardi.** *KAHR-dee.* Chards.

1086. **Carote.** *kah-RAW-tay.* Carrots.

1087. Cavolfiori. *kah-vohl-FYOH-ree.* Cauliflower.

1088. Cavoli. *KAH-vo-lee.* Cabbage.

1089. Ceci. *CHAY-chee.* Chick peas.

1090. Cetriolo. *chay-tree-AW-lo.* Cucumber.

1091. Cipolle. *chee-POHL-lay.* Onions.

1092. Fagioli. *fah-JAW-lee.* Beans.

1093. Fagiolini. *fah-jo-LEE-nee.* String beans.

1094. Fave. *FAH-vay.* A kind of lima beans.

1095. Finocchi. *fee-NAWK-kee.* Fennel.

1096. Funghi. *FOON-gee.* Mushrooms.

1097. Insalata. *een-sah-LAH-tah.* Salad.

1098. Lattuga. *laht-TOO-gah.* Lettuce.

1099. Lenticchie. *layn-TEEK-kyay.* Lentils.

1100. Melanzane. *may-lahn-TSAH-nay.* Egg plant.

1101. Patate. *pah-TAH-tay.* Potatoes.

1102. Patata al forno. *pah-TAH-tah ahl FOHR-no.* Baked potato.

1103. Patata bollita. *pah-TAH-tah bohl-LEE-tah.* Boiled potato.

1104. Puré di patate. *poo-REH dee pah-TAH-tay.* Mashed potatoes.

1105. Patate fritte. *pah-TAH-tay FREET-tay.* Fried potatoes.

1106. Peperoni. *pay-pay-RO-nee.* Peppers.

1107. Piselli. *pee-SEL-lee.* Peas.

1108. Pomodori. *po-mo-DAW-ree.* Tomatoes.

1109. Pomodori ripieni. *po-mo-DAW-ree ree-PYEH-nee.* Stuffed tomatoes.

1110. Rape. *RAH-pay.* Turnips.

1111. **Scarola.** *skah-RAW-lah.* Escarole.

1112. **Sedano.** *SEH-dah-no.* Celery.

1113. **Sedano e olive.** *SEH-dah-no ay o-LEE-vay.* Celery and olives.

1114. **Spinaci.** *spee-NAH-chee.* Spinach.

1115. **Tartufi.** *tahr-TOO-fee.* Truffles.

1116. **Zucca.** *TSOOK-kah.* Squash.

1117. **Zucchini.** *tsook-KEE-nee.* "Zucchini" squash.

SEASONINGS
CONDIMENTI

1118. **L'aceto.** *lah-CHAY-toh.* The vinegar.

1119. **L'aglio.** *LAH-lyoh.* The garlic.

1120. **L'olio.** *LAW-lyoh.* The oil.

1121. **Il pepe.** *eel PAY-pay.* The pepper.

1122. **La rubra.** *lah ROO-brah.* The catsup.

1123. **Il sale.** *eel SAH-lay.* The salt.

1124. **La senapa.** *lah SEH-nah-pah.* The mustard.

1125. **Il sugo.** *eel SOO-go.* The sauce.

1126. **Lo zucchero.** *lo DZOOK-kay-ro.* The sugar.

DESSERTS
DOLCI

1127. **Amaretti.** *ah-mah-RAYT-tee.* Small macaroons.

1128. **Bignè.** *bee-NYEH.* Cream puff.

1129. **Biscotti.** *bee-SKAWT-tee.* Cookies.

1130. Brigidini. *bree-jee-DEE-nee.* Aniseed wafers.

1131. Buccellato. *booch-chayl-LAH-toh.* Cake in the shape of rings or rolls (made with pastry flour, sugar, vanilla, aniseed and currants).

1132. Budino. *boo-DEE-no.* Pudding.

1133. Cannoli. *kahn-NAW-lee.* Rolls of pastry filled with ricotta. (Sicilian specialty.)

1134. Caramelle. *kah-rah-MEL-lay.* Hard candies.

1135. Cassata alla siciliana. *kahs-SAH-tah AHL-lah see-chee-LYAH-nah.* Spumone. (A kind of ice cream or cake made of buttermilk, sugar, vanilla, chocolate, candied fruits and sweet liqueur.)

1136. Castagnaccio. *kah-stah-NYAHCH-chyoh.* Pancakes (made of chestnut flour, pine-nuts and currants).

1137. Ciambelle. *chyahm-BEL-lay.* Doughnuts.

1138. Cotognata. *ko-toh-NYAH-tah.* Quince paste.

1139. Crema. KREH-mah. Custard.

1140. Croccanti. *krohk-KAHN-tee.* Almond cookies.

1141. Crostata. *kro-STAH-tah.* Pie.

1142. Dolce. *DOHL-chay.* Dessert.

1143. Frittelle. *freet-TEL-lay.* Rings of dough fried, sprinkled with sugar and served hot, similar to crullers.

1144. Gelato di cioccolata. *jay-LAH-toh dee chyohk-ko-LAH-tah.* Chocolate ice cream.

1145. Gelato di crema. *jay-LAH-toh dee KREH-mah.* Vanilla ice cream.

1146. Granita. *grah-NEE-tah.* Ice.

1147. Granita al limone. *grah-NEE-tah ahl lee-MO-nay.* Lemon ice.

1148. Granita di caffè. *grah-NEE-tah dee kahf-FEH.* Coffee ice.

1149. Macedonia di frutta. *mah-chay-DAW-nyah dee FROOT-tah.* Fruit cup in wine syrup.

1150. Mandorle tostate. *MAHN-dohr-lay toh-STAH-tay.* Almond praline.

1151. Maritozzi. *mah-ree-TAWT-tsee.* Large, sweet buns.

1152. Marmellata di cotogne. *mahr-mayl-LAH-tah dee ko-TOH-nyay.* Quince jam.

1153. Mele fritte al rum. *MAY-lay FREET-tay ahl room.* Fried apples with rum.

1154. Monte bianco. *MOHN-tay BYAHN-ko.* A sweet made of chestnuts, brandy and whipped cream.

1155. Mostaccioli. *mo-stahch-CHYAW-lee.* Small sweet cakes of almonds, chocolate and candied fruits.

1156. Pan di Spagna. *pahn dee SPAH-nyah.* Sponge cake.

1157. Panettone. *pah-nay-TOH-nay.* Fruit cake made of fine flour mixed with eggs, sugar, butter and candied fruit peel. (Specialty of Milan.)

1158. Panforte di Siena. *pahn-FAWR-tay dee SYEH-nah.* A hard sweet from Siena.

1159. Panna montata. *PAHN-nah mohn-TAH-tah.* Whipped cream.

1160. Pasta alla frutta. *PAH-stah AHL-lah FROOT-tah.* Fruit tart.

1161. **Pasta frolla.** *PAH-stah FRAWL-lah.* Short bread.

1162. **Paste.** *PAH-stay.* Pastry.

1163. **Savoiardi.** *sah-vo-YAHR-dee.* Lady fingers.

1164. **Sfingi.** *SFEEN-jee.* Small cakes or cookies.

1165. **Sfogliatella.** *sfoh-lyah-TEL-lah.* Light pastry.

1166. **Sorbetto.** *sohr-BAYT-toh.* Fruit ice.

1167. **Spumone.** *spoo-MO-nay.* Italian ice cream.

1168. **Torrone.** *tohr-RO-nay.* Nougat made of honey, almonds and nuts.

1169. **Torta di frutta.** *TOHR-tah dee FROOT-tah.* Pie.

1170. **Torta di ricotta.** *TOHR-tah dee ree-KAWT-tah.* Cheese cake.

1171. **Zabaglione.** *dzah-bah-LYOH-nay.* Light custard of egg-nog flavor (made of egg yolks, sugar, wine and served hot or cold).

1172. **Zeppole.** *TSAYP-po-lay.* Sweet dough fritters.

1173. **Zuppa inglese.** *TSOOP-pah een-GLAY-say.* Rum cake.

CHEESES
FORMAGGI

1174. **Bel Paese.** *bel pah_AY-zay.* A semi-soft cheese of creamy quality, delicate in flavor and slightly salted.

1175. **Caciocavallo.** *kah-chyoh-kah-VAHL-lo.* An Italian cheese from the South, of elongated shape similar to provolone.

1176. Gorgonzola.   *gohr-gohn-DZAW-lah.*   Green, soft and translucent cheese of piquant flavor due to the cultivation of a special mould.

1177. Groviera.   *gro-VYEH-rah.*   Swiss cheese.

1178. Mascarpone.   *mah-skahr-PO-nay.*   A kind of cottage cheese from Lombardy, made with cream.

1179. Mozzarella.   *moht-tsah-REL-lah.*   White, soft, delicate cheese made of cow's milk.

1180. Parmigiano.   *pahr-mee-JAH-no.*   A granulous cheese, spotted with light yellow color and aromatic in flavor.

1181. Pecorino.   *pay-ko-REE-no.*   Salty, piquant cheese made of sheep milk.

1182. Provola.   *PRAW-vo-lah.*   Fresh cheese similar to mozzarella.

1183. Provolone.   *pro-vo-LO-nay.*   Hard, round cheese from Southern Italy.

1184. Ricotta.   *ree-KAWT-tah.*   A variety of cottage cheese produced by the repeated boiling of skimmed milk.

1185. Robiola.   *ro-BYAW-lah.*   Sweet, fresh cheese made of sheep or goat's milk.

1186. Stracchino.   *strahk-KEE-no.*   Buttery, non-fermented cheese from Lombardy, made of cow's milk.

FRUITS
FRUTTA

1187. Arancio.   *ah-RAHN-chyoh.*   Orange.

1188. Ciliege.   *chee-LYEH-jay.*   Cherries.

1189. Fragole.   *FRAH-go-lay.*   Strawberries.

1190. Lamponi.   *lahm-P̱O-nee.*   Raspberries.

1191. Limone.   *lee-MO-nay.*   Lemon.

1192. Mela.   *MAY-lah.*   Apple.

1193. Melone.   *may-LO-nay.*   Melon.

1194. Pesca.   *PEH-skah.*   Peach.

1195. Pompelmo.   *pohm-PEL-mo.*   Grapefruit.

1196. Uva.   *OO-vah.*   Grapes.

BEVERAGES
BEVANDE

1197. Acqua minerale.   *AHK-kwah mee-nay-RAH-lay*
Mineral water.

1198. Aranciata.   *ah-rahn-CHYAH-tah.*   Orangeade.

1199. Bibita.   *BEE-bee-tah.*   Any soft drink.

1200. Caffè e latte.   *kahf-FEH ay LAHT-tay.*   Coffee
with milk.

1201. Caffè espresso.   *kahf-FEH ays-PRES-so.*
Italian coffee (made by forcing steam through
Italian black coffee).

1202. Caffè nero.   *kahf-FEH NAY-ro.*   Black coffee.

1203. **Succo di frutta.** *SOOK-ko dee FROOT-tah.*
Fruit juice.

1204. **Cioccolata calda.** *chyohk-ko-LAH-tah KAHL-dah.* Hot chocolate.

1205. **Limonata.** *lee-mo-NAH-tah.* Lemonade.

1206. **Latte.** *LAHT-tay.* Milk.

1207. **Tè.** *teh.* Tea.

CHURCH

IN CHIESA

1208. **At what time is the [service] mass?**
A che ora c'è [la funzione] la messa?
ah kay O-rah cheh [lah foon-TSYOH-nay] lah MAYS-sah?

1209. **A Catholic church.**
Una chiesa cattolica.
OO-nah KYEH-zah kaht-TAW-lee-kah.

1210. **A Protestant church.**
Una chiesa protestante.
OO-nah KYEH-zah pro-tay-STAHN-tay.

1211. **A synagogue.**
Una sinagoga.
OO-nah see-nah-GAW-gah.

1212. **Is there a [priest] rabbi, minister who speaks English?**
C'è un [prete] rabbino, pastore protestante che parla l'inglese?
cheh oon [PREH-tay] rahb-BEE-no, pah-STO-ray pro-tay-STAHN-tay kay PAHR-lah leen-GLAY-say?

SIGHTSEEING

GIRO TURISTICO

1213. Where can I rent [a car]?
Dove posso noleggiare [una macchina]?
DOH-vay PAWS-so no-layj-JAH-ray [OO-nah MAHK-kee-nah]?

1214. —— a bicycle.
una bicicletta.
OO-nah bee-chee-KLAYT-tah.

1215. —— a horse and carriage.
una carrozza.
OO-nah kahr-RAWT-tsah.

1216. I want a licensed guide who speaks English.
Vorrei una guida patentata che parli l'inglese.
vohr-REH_ee OO-nah GWEE-dah pah-tayn-TAH-tah kay PAHR-lee leen-glay-say.

1217. What is the charge [per hour] per day?
Quanto si paga [all'ora] al giorno?
KWAHN-toh see PAH-gah [ahl-LO-rah] ahl JOHR-no?

1218. How much does a ticket cost?
Quanto costa il biglietto?
KWAHN-toh KAW-stah eel bee-LYAYT-toh?

1219. Can one go [to the island]?
Si può andare [all'isola]?
see pwaw ahn-DAH-ray [ahl-LEE-zo-lah]?

1220. —— to the mountains.
in montagna.
een mohn-TAH-nyah.

1221. —— **to the sea.**
    al mare.
    ahl MAH-ray.

1222. —— **Can one go up the river?**
    Si può risalire il fiume?
    see pwaw ree-sah-LEE-ray eel FYOO-may?

1223. **Call for me tomorrow at 8 o'clock at my hotel.**
    Venga a prendermi all'albergo domani alle otto.
    VEN-gah ah PREN-dayr-mee ahl-lahl-BEHR-go doh-MAH-nee AHL-lay AWT-toh.

1224. **Please show me all the sights of interest.**
    Per favore mi faccia vedere tutte le cose interessanti.
    payr fah-VO-ray mee FAHCH-chyah vay-DAY-ray TOOT-tay lay KAW-say een-tay-rays-SAHN-tee.

1225. **I am interested in [architecture].**
    Mi interesso di [architettura].
    mee een-tay-RES-so dee [ahr-kee-tayt-TOO-rah].

1226. —— **painting.**
    pittura.
    peet-TOO-rah.

1227. —— **sculpture.**
    scultura.
    skool-TOO-rah.

1228. **I am interested in native arts and crafts.**
    Mi interessa l'artigianato.
    mee een-tay-RES-sah lahr-tee-jah-NAH-toh.

1229. **I would like to visit [the park].**
    Mi piacerebbe visitare [il parco].
    mee pyah-chay-REB-bay vee-zee-TAH-ray [eel PAHR-ko]

1230. —— **the cathedral.**
la cattedrale.
lah kaht-tay-DRAH-lay.

1231. —— **the castle.**
il castello.
eel kah-STEL-lo.

1232. —— **the library.**
la biblioteca.
lah bee-blyoh-TEH-kah.

1233. —— **the monument.**
il monumento.
eel mo-noo-MAYN-toh.

1234. —— **the palace.**
il palazzo.
eel pah-LAHT-tso.

1235. At what time does the museum [open] close?
A che ora si [apre] chiude il museo?
ah kay O-rah see [AH-pray] KYOO-day eel moo-ZEH-o?

1236. Is this the way to [the entrance] the exit?
Si va di qui [all'entrata] all'uscita?
see vah dee kwee [ahl-layn-TRAH-tah] ahl-loo-SHEE-tah?

1237. What is the price of admission?
Quanto costa il biglietto d'entrata?
KWAHN-toh KAW-stah eel bee-LYAYT-toh dayn-TRAH-tah?

1238. We would like to stop and see the view.
Ci piacerebbe fermarci e guardare il panorama.
chee pyah-chay-REB-bay fayr-MAHR-chee ay gwahr-DAH-ray eel pah-no-RAH-mah.

1239. Please take us back to the hotel.
Per favore ci riporti all'albergo.
payr fah-VO-ray chee ree-PAWR-tee ahl-ahl-BEHR-go.

1240. If we have time, we shall visit the art gallery.
Se abbiamo tempo, visiteremo la galleria d'arte.
say ahb-BYAH-mo TEM-po, vee-zee-tay-RAY-mo lah gahl-lay-REE-ah DAHR-tay.

AMUSEMENTS
DIVERTIMENTI

1241. I would like to go·[to a concert].
Mi piacerebbe andare [ad un concerto].
mee pyah-chay-REB-bay ahn-DAH-ray [ahd oon kohn-CHEHR-toh].

1242. —— to the ballet.
al balletto.
ahl bahl-LAYT-toh.

1243. —— to the box office.
al botteghino del teatro.
ahl boht-tay-GEE-no dayl tay-AH-tro.

1244. —— to the gambling casino.
al casino.
ahl kah-SEE-no.

1245. —— to the movies.
al cinematografo.
ahl chee-nay-mah-TAW-grah-fo.

1246. —— **to see the folk dances.**
a vedere le danze in costume.
ah vay-DAY-ray lay DAHN-tsay een ko-STOO-may.

1247. —— **to a night club.**
ad un cabaret.
ahd oon kah-bah-RAY.

1248. —— **to the opera.**
all'opera.
ahl-LAW-pay-rah.

1249. —— **to the theater.**
a teatro.
ah tay-AH-tro.

1250. What are they showing tonight?
Che cosa danno stasera?
kay KAW-sah DAHN-no stah-SAY-rah?

1251. How much is [an orchestra seat]?
Quanto costa [una poltrona di platea]?
KWAHN-toh KAW-stah [OO-nah pohl-TRO-nah dee plah-TEH-ah]?

1252. —— **a balcony seat.**
un posto in galleria.
oon PO-stoh een gahl-lay-REE-ah.

1253. —— **a box.**
un palco.
oon PAHL-ko.

1254. May I have a program?
Potrei avere un programma?
po-TREH_ee ah-VAY-ray oon pro-GRAHM-mah?

1255. Can I rent opera glasses?
Posso affittare un binoccolo?
PAWS-so ahf-feet-TAH-ray oon bee-NAWK-ko-lo?

1256. Is there a matinee performance today?

C'è una rappresentazione diurna oggi?

cheh OO-nah rahp-pray-sayn-tah-TSYOH-nay dee-OOR-nah AWJ-jee?

1257. Have you any seats for tonight?

Ha dei posti per stasera?

ah day PO-stee payr stah-SAY-rah?

1258. Not [too near] too far away from the stage.

Non [troppo vicino al] troppo lontano dal palco-scenico.

nawn [TRAWP-po vee-CHEE-no ahl] TRAWP-po lohn-TAH-no dahl pahl-ko-SHEH-nee-ko.

1259. Will I be able [to see] hear well?

Potrò [vedere] sentire bene?

po-TRAW [vay-DAY-ray] sayn-TEE-ray BEH-nay?

1260. What time does [the evening performance] the floor show begin?

A che ora comincia [lo spettacolo serale] lo spettacolo di sala?

ah kay O-rah ko-MEEN-chyah [lo spet-TAH-ko-lo say-RAH-lay] lo spet-TAH-ko-lo dee SAH-lah?

1261. How long is the intermission?

Quanto dura l'intervallo?

KWAHN-toh DOO-rah leen-tayr-VAHL-lo?

1262. The show was [interesting] funny.

Lo spettacolo è stato [interessante] divertente.

lo spayt-TAH-ko-lo eh STAH-toh [een-tay-rays-SAHN-tay] dee-vayr-TEN-tay.

1263. Is there a cover charge?

Si paga qualcosa per il coperto?

see PAH-gah kwahl-KAW-sah payr eel ko-PEHR-toh?

1264. Where can we go to dance?
Dove possiamo andare a ballare?
DOH-vay pohs-SYAH-mo ahn-DAH-ray ah bahl-LAH-ray?

1265. May I have this dance?
Posso invitarla per questa danza?
PAWS-so een-vee-TAHR-lah payr KWAY-stah DAHN-tsah?

1266. Will you play [a fox trot]?
Vuol suonare [un "fox trot"]?
vwawl swaw-NAH-ray [oon "fox trot"]?

1267. —— a mambo.
un mambo.
oon "mambo."

1268. —— a rumba.
una rumba.
OO-nah ROOM-bah.

1269. —— a samba.
una samba.
OO-nah "samba."

1270. —— a tango.
un tango.
oon TAHN-go.

1271. —— a waltz.
un valzer.
oon VAHL-tsayr.

1272. The music is excellent.
La musica è ottima.
lah MOO-zee-kah eh AWT-tee-mah.

SPORTS

SPORT

1273. Let's go [to the beach].
Andiamo [alla spiaggia].
ahn-DYAH-mo [AHL-lah SPYAHJ-jah].

1274. —— to the swimming pool.
alla piscina.
AHL-lah pee-SHEE-nah.

1275. —— to the soccer game.
alla partita di calcio.
AHL-lah pahr-TEE-tah dee KAHL-chyoh.

1276. —— to the automobile races.
alla corsa automobilistica.
AHL-lah KAWR-sah ah̬oo-toh-moh-bee-LEE-stee-kah.

1277. —— to the horse races.
alle corse dei cavalli.
AHL-lay KOHR-say day kah-VAHL-lee.

1278. I'd like to play [golf] tennis.
Mi piacerebbe giocare [al golf] a tennis.
mee pyah-chay-REB-bay jo-KAH-ray [ahl gohlf] ah TEN-nees.

1279. I need [some golf clubs].
Ho bisogno di [bastoni per il golf].
aw bee-ZO-nyoh dee [bah-STO-nee payr eel gohlf].

1280. —— a tennis racket.
una racchetta da tennis.
OO-nah rahk-KAYT-tah dah TEN-nees.

1281. —— **some fishing tackle.**
 alcuni attrezzi per la pesca.
 ahl-KOO-nee aht-TRAYT-tsee payr lah PAY-skah.

1282. **Can we go [fishing]?**
 Possiamo andare [a pescare]?
 pohs-SYAH-mo ahn-DAH-ray [ah PAY-skah-ray]?

1283. —— **horseback riding.**
 a cavallo.
 ah kah-VAHL-lo.

1284. —— **swimming.**
 a nuotare.
 ah nwaw-TAH-ray.

1285. —— **skating.**
 a pattinare.
 ah paht-tee-NAH-ray.

1286. —— **skiing.**
 a sciare.
 ah shee-AH-ray.

BANK AND MONEY
OPERAZIONI BANCARIE

1287. **Where is the nearest bank?**
 Dov'è la banca più vicina?
 doh-VEH lah BAHN-kah pyoo vee-CHEE-nah?

1288. **At which window can I cash this?**
 A quale sportello posso riscuotere questo?
 ah KWAH-lay spohr-TEL-lo PAWS-so ree-SKWAW-tay-ray KWAY-sto?

1289. Will you cash a check for me?
Mi può riscuotere un assegno?
mee pwaw ree-SKWAW-tay-ray oon ahs-SAY-nyoh?

1290. I have [traveler's checks].
Ho dei [traveler's checks].
aw day ["traveler's checks"].

1291. —— a bank draft.
un vaglia bancario.
oon VAH-lyah bahn-KAH-ryoh.

1292. —— a letter of credit.
una lettera di credito.
OO-nah LET-tay-rah dee KRAY-dee-toh.

1293. —— a credit card.
un buono d'accredito.
oon BWAW-no dahk-KRAY-dee-toh.

1294. What is the exchange rate on the dollar?
Qual'è il cambio del dollaro?
kwah-LEH eel KAHM-byoh dayl DAWL-lah-ro?

1295. May I have thirty dollars' worth of lire?
Posso avere trenta dollari in lire?
PAWS-so ah-VAY-ray TRAYN-tah DAWL-lah-ree een LEE-ray?

1296. Please change this for [some large bills].
Per favore mi cambi questo con [delle banconote di grosso taglio].
payr fah-VO-ray mee KAHM-bee KWAY-sto kohn [DAYL-lay bahn-ko-NO-tay dee GRAWS-so TAH-lyoh].

1297. —— some small bills.
delle banconote di piccolo taglio.
DAYL-lay bahn-ko-NO-tay dee PEEK-ko-lo TAH-lyoh.

1298. Give me some small change.
Mi dia degli spiccioli.
mee DEE-ah DAY-lyee SPEECH-chyoh-lee.

1299. I want to send fifty dollars to the U.S.
Voglio mandare cinquanta dollari negli Stati
Uniti.
*VAW-lyoh mahn-DAH-ray cheen-KWAHN-tah
DAWL-lah-ree NAY-lyee STAH-tee oo-NEE-
tee.*

SHOPPING

COMPERE

1300. I want to do some shopping.
Vorrei andare a fare delle spese.
*vohr-REH_ee ahn-DAH-ray ah FAH-ray DAYL-lay
SPAY-say.*

1301. Please take me to the shopping section.
Per favore mi accompagni al quartiere dei
negozi.
*payr fah-VO-ray mee ahk-kohm-PAH-nyee ahl
kwahr-TYEH-ray day nay-GAW-tsee.*

1302. May I speak to a [salesman] salesgirl.
Potrei parlare con [un commesso] una commessa.
*po-TREH_ee pahr-LAH-ray kohn [oon kohm-MAYS-
so] OO-nah kohm-MAYS-sah.*

1303. Is there an English-speaking person here?
C'è qualcuno qui che parla l'inglese?
*cheh kwahl-KOO-no kwee kay PAHR-lah leen-GLAY-
say?*

1304. I am just looking around.
Sto guardando.
sto gwahr-DAHN-doh.

1305. Sale.
Vendita.
VAYN-dee-tah.

1306. How much is it [for each piece]?/
Quanto costa [al pezzo]?
KWAHN-toh KAW-stah [ahl PET-tso]?

1307. —— per meter.
al metro.
ahl MEH-tro.

1308. —— all together.
tutto insieme.
TOOT-toh een-SYEH-may.

1309. It is too expensive.
È troppo caro.
eh TRAWP-po KAH-ro.

1310. Is that the best price that you can give me?
È il prezzo migliore che mi può fare?
eh eel PRET-tso mee-LYOH-ray kay mee pwaw FAH-ray?

1311. Is there [a discount] a guarantee?
C'è [uno sconto] una garanzia?
cheh [OO-no SKOHN-toh] OO-nah gah-rahn-TSEE-ah?

1312. The price is satisfactory.
Il prezzo va bene.
eel PRET-tso vah BEH-nay.

1313. I (do not) like that.
(Non) mi piace quello.
(nawn) mee PYAH-chay KWAYL-lo.

1314. I would prefer something [better].
Preferirei qualche cosa [di migliore].
pray-fay-ree-REH_ee KWAHL-kay KAW-sah [dee mee-LYOH-ray].

1315. —— cheaper.
di meno caro.
dee MAY-no KAH-ro.

1316. —— at a moderate price.
più a buon mercato.
pyoo ah·bwawn mayr-KAH-toh.

1317. —— finer.
di più fine.
dee pyoo FEE-nay.

1318. —— plainer.
di più semplice.
dee pyoo SAYM-plee-chay.

1319. —— softer.
di più soffice.
dee pyoo SAWF-fee-chay.

1320. —— stronger.
di più forte.
dee pyoo FAWR-tay.

1321. —— looser.
di più largo.
dee pyoo LAHR-go.

1322. —— tighter.
di più stretto.
dee pyoo STRAYT-toh.

1323. —— of medium size.
di misura media.
dee mee-ZOO-rah MEH-dyah.

1324. Show me some others in a different style.

Me ne mostri degli altri di stile diverso.

may nay MO-stree DAY-lyee AHL-tree dee STEE-lay dee-VEHR-so.

1325. May I try it on?

Posso provarlo?

PAWS-so pro-VAHR-lo?

1326. Will it [fade] shrink?

Si [scolorirà] restringerà?

see [sko-lo-ree-RAH] ray-streen-jay-RAH?

1327. It is (not) becoming to me.

(Non) mi sta bene.

(nawn) mee stah BEH-nay.

1328. Can I order one of them?

Ne posso ordinare uno?

nay PAWS-so ohr-dee-NAH-ray OO-no?

1329. How long will the alterations take?

Quanto tempo ci vuole per aggiustarlo?

KWAHN-toh TEM-po chee VWAW-lay payr ahj-joo-STAHR-lo?

1330. I shall come back [later] soon.

Ritornerò [più tardi] tra poco.

ree-tohr-nay-RAW [pyoo TAHR-dee] trah PAW-ko.

1331. Please wrap this.

Per favore m'impacchi questo.

payr fah-VO-ray meem-PAHK-kee KWAY-sto.

1332. I shall take it with me.

Lo porto con me.

lo PAWR-toh kohn may.

1333. Whom do I pay? The cashier?

Chi pago? Il cassiere?

kee PAH-go? eel kahs-SYEH-ray?

1334. Can you deliver it to my hotel?
Può mandarlo al mio albergo?
pwaw mahn-DAHR-lo ahl MEE-o ahl-BEHR-go?

1335. It is fragile.
È fragile.
eh FRAH-jee-lay.

1336. Pack it for export.
L'impacchi per l'esportazione.
leem-PAHK-kee payr lay-spohr-tah-TSYOH-nay.

1337. Ship it to Philadelphia.
Lo spedisca a Philadelphia.
lo spay-DEE-skah ah Philadelphia.

1338. Please give me [the bill].
Per favore mi dia [il conto].
payr fah-VO-ray mee DEE-ah [eel KOHN-toh].

1339. —— a receipt.
una ricevuta.
OO-nah ree-chay-VOO-tah.

1340. —— a sales slip.
uno scontrino di vendita.
OO-no skohn-TREE-no dee VAYN-dee-tah.

1341. You will be paid on delivery.
Sarete pagato alla consegna.
sah-RAY-tay pah-GAH-toh AHL-lah kohn-SAY-nyah.

1342. Are there any other charges?
C'è da pagare altro?
cheh dah pah-GAH-ray AHL-tro?

MEASUREMENTS

MISURE

1343. Please take my measurements.
Per favore mi prenda le misure.
payr fah-VO-ray mee PREN-dah lay mee-ZOO-ray.

1344. What is [the size]?
Qual'è [la misura]?
kwah-LEH [lah mee-ZOO-rah]?

1345. —— the length.
la lunghezza.
lah loon-GAYT-tsah.

1346. —— the width.
la larghezza.
lah lahr-GAYT-tsah.

1347. —— the weight.
il peso.
eel PAY-so.

1348. It is 7 meters long by 4 meters wide.
È sette metri di lunghezza per quattro di
larghezza.
*eh SET-tay MAY-tree dee loon-GAYT-tsah payr
KWAHT-tro dee lahr-GAYT-tsah.*

1349. Small.   **Smaller.**
Piccolo.   Più piccolo.
PEEK-ko-lo.   *pyoo PEEK-ko-lo.*

1350. Large.   **Larger.**
Grande.   Più grande.
GRAHN-day.   *pyoo GRAHN-day.*

1351. High
Alto.
AHL-toh.

Higher.
Più alto.
pyoo AHL-toh.

1352. Low
Basso.
BAHS-so.

Lower.
Più basso.
pyoo BAHS-so.

1353. Long.
Lungo.
LOON-go.

Longer.
Più lungo.
pyoo LOON-go.

1354. Short.
Corto.
KOHR-toh.

Shorter.
Più corto.
pyoo KOHR-toh.

1355. Thin.
Sottile.
soht-TEE-lay.

Thinner.
Più sottile.
pyoo soht-TEE-lay.

1356. Thick.
Grosso.
GRAWS-so.

Thicker.
Più grosso.
pyoo GRAWS-so.

1357. Narrow.
Stretto.
STRAYT-toh.

Narrower.
Più stretto.
pyoo STRAYT-toh.

1358. Wide.
Largo.
LAHR-go.

Wider.
Più largo.
pyoo LAHR-go.

1359. Old.
Vecchio.
VEK-kyoh.

Older.
Più vecchio.
pyoo VEK-kyoh.

1360. New.
Nuovo.
NWAW-vo.

Newer.
Più nuovo.
pyoo NWAW-vo.

COLORS
COLORI

1361. I want a [lighter] darker shade.
Voglio una tinta [più chiara] più scura.
*VAW-lyoh OO-nah TEEN-tah [pyoo KYAH-rah]
pyoo SKOO-rah.*

1362. Black. Nero. *NAY-ro.*

1363. Blue. Azzurro. *ahd-DZOO-ro.*

1364. Brown. Marrone. *mahr-RO-nay.*

1365. Cream. Beige. *behj.*

1366. Gray. Grigio. *GREE-jo.*

1367. Green. Verde. *VAYR-day.*

1368. Orange. Arancione. *ah-rahn-CHYOH-nay.*

1369. Pink. Rosa. *RAW-zah.*

1370. Purple. Violetto. *vyoh-LAYT-toh.*

1371. Red. Rosso. *ROHS-so.*

1372. White. Bianco. *BYAHN-ko.*

1373. Yellow. Giallo. *JAHL-lo.*

STORES
NEGOZI

1374. Can you direct me to [an antique shop]?
Mi può indicare [un antiquario]?
*mee pwaw een-dee-KAH-ray [oon ahn-tee-KWAH-
ryoh]?*

1375. —— a bakery. una panetteria.
OO-nah pah-nayt-tay-REE-ah.

1376. ——a bookshop. una libreria.
OO-nah lee-bray-REE-ah.

1377. —— **a butcher.** una macelleria.
OO-nah mah-chayl-lay-REE-ah.

1378. —— **a candy store.** una confetteria.
OO-nah kohn-fayt-tay-REE-ah.

1379. —— **a cigar store.** un tabaccaio.
oon tah-bahk-KAH-yoh.

1380. —— **a clothing store.** un negozio di vestiario.
oon nay-GAW-tsyoh dee vay-STYAH-ryoh.

1381. —— **a department store.** un magazzino.
oon mah-gahd-DZEE-no.

1382. —— **a dressmaker.** una sartoria.
OO-nah sahr-toh-REE-ah.

1383. —— **a drug store.** una farmacia.
OO-nah fahr-mah-CHEE-ah.

1384. —— **a five and dime store.**
un magazzino a prezzo fisso.
oon mah-gahd-DZEE-no ah PRET-tso FEES-so.

1385. —— **a florist.** un fioraio.
oon fyoh-RAH-yoh.

1386. —— **a fruit and vegetable store.**
un negozio di frutta e verdura.
oon nay-GAW-tsyoh dee FROOT-tah ay vayr-DOO-rah.

1387. —— **a grocery.**
un negozio di generi alimentari.
oon nay-GAW-tsyoh dee JAH-nay-ree ah-lee-mayn-TAH-ree.

1388. —— **a hardware store.**
un negozio di articoli domestici.
oon nay-GAW-tsyoh dee ahr-TEE-ko-lee doh-MEH-stee-chee.

1389. —— **a hat shop.**   una cappelleria.
OO-nah kahp-payl-lay-REE-ah.

1390. —— **a jewelry store.**   una gioielleria.
OO-nah jo-yayl-lay-REE-ah.

1391. —— **a liquor store.**
una rivendita di liquori.
OO-nah ree-VAYN-dee-tah dee lee-KWAW-ree.

1392. —— **a market.**   un mercato.
oon mayr-KAH-toh.

1393. —— **a meat market.**   una macelleria.
OO-nah mah-chayl-lay-REE-ah.

1394. —— **a milliner.**   una modisteria.
OO-nah mo-dee-stay-REE-ah.

1395. —— **a music shop.**   un negozio di musica.
oon nay-GAW-tsyoh dee MOO-zee-kah.

1396. —— **a shoe repair shop.**   un calzolaio.
oon kahl-tso-LAH-yoh.

1397. —— **a shoe store.**   una calzoleria.
OO-nah kahl-tso-lay-REE-ah.

1398. —— **a tailor.**   un sarto.   *oon SAHR-toh.*

1399. —— **a toy shop.**   un negozio di giocattoli.
oon nay-GAW-tsyoh dee jo-KAHT-toh-lee.

1400. —— **a watchmaker.**   un orologiaio.
oon o-ro-lo-JAH-yoh.

1401. —— **a haberdasher.**
un negozio di abbigliamento da uomo.
*oon nay-GAW-tsyoh dee ahb-bee-lyah-MAYN-
toh dah WAW-mo.*

CIGAR STORE
IL TABACCAIO

1402. Is the cigar store open?
È aperto il tabaccaio?
eh ah-PEHR-toh eel tah-bahk-KAH-yoh?

1403. I want to buy [some cigars].
Vorrei comprare [dei sigari].
vohr-REH_ee kohm-PRAH-ray [day SEE-gah-ree].

1404. —— a pack of American cigarettes.
un pacchetto di sigarette americane.
*oon pahk-KAYT-toh dee see-gah-RAYT-tay
ah-may-ree-KAH-nay.*

1405. —— a cigarette case (leather).
un portasigarette (di cuoio).
oon pohr-tah-see-gah-RAYT-tay (dee KWAW-yoh).

1406. —— a pipe.
una pipa.
OO-nah PEE-pah.

1407. —— some pipe tobacco.
del tabacco da pipa.
dayl tah-BAHK-ko dah PEE-pah.

1408. —— a lighter.
un accendisigari.
oon ahch-chayn-dee-SEE-gah-ree.

1409. —— some lighter fluid.
della benzina.
DAYL-lah bayn-DZEE-nah.

1410. —— a flint.
un acciarino.
oon ahch-chyah-REE-no.

DRUGSTORE

LA FARMACIA

1411. Where is there a drugstore where they understand English?
Dov'è una farmacia dove capiscono l'inglese?
doh-VEH OO-nah fahr-mah-CHEE-ah DOH-vay kah-PEE-sko-no leen-GLAY-say?

1412. Can you fill this prescription immediately?
Mi può preparare questa ricetta subito?
mee pwaw pray-pah-RAH-ray KWAY-stah ree-CHET-tah SOO-bee-toh?

1413. Do you have [some adhesive tape]?
Ha [del nastro adesivo]?
ah [dayl NAH-stro ah-day-ZEE-vo]?

1414. —— some alcohol. dell'alcool.
dayl-LAHL-kawl.

1415. —— an antiseptic. del disinfettante.
dayl dee-zeen-fayt-TAHN-tay.

1416. —— some aspirin. dell'aspirina.
dayl-lah-spee-REE-nah.

1417. —— some bandages. delle fasciature.
DAYL-lay fah-shyah-TOO-ray.

1418. —— some bicarbonate of soda.
del bicarbonato di soda.
dayl bee-kahr-bo-NAH-toh dee SAW-dah.

1419. —— some boric acid. dell'acido borico.
dayl-LAH-chee-doh BAW-ree-ko.

1420. —— a jar of cold cream.
un vasetto di crema per la pelle.
oon vah-ZAYT-toh dee KREH-mah payr lah PEL-lay.

1421. —— **a comb.** un pettine. *oon PET-tee-nay.*

1422. —— **some corn pads.** del callifugo.
    dayl kahl-LEE-foo-go.

1423. —— **a deodorant.** del deodorante.
    dayl day-oh-doh-RAHN-tay.

1424. —— **a depilatory.** un depilatore.
    oon day-pee-lah-TOH-ray.

1425. —— **some ear stoppers.**
    dei tamponi da orecchi.
    day tahm-PO-nee dah o-RAYK-kee.

1426. —— **an eyecup.** una coppetta per gli occhi.
    OO-nah kohp-PAYT-tah payr lyee AWK-kee.

1427. —— **a box of face tissues.**
    una scatola di fazzoletti di carta.
    *OO-nah SKAH-toh-lah dee faht-tso-LAYT-tee
    dee KAHR-tah.*

1428. —— **some gauze.** della garza.
    DAYL-lah GAHR-dzah.

1429. —— **some hand lotion.**
    della lozione per le mani.
    DAYL-lah lo-TSYOH-nay payr lay MAH-nee.

1430. —— **a hairbrush.** una spazzola per i capelli.
    OO-nah SPAHT-tso-lah payr ee kah-PAYL-lee.

1431. —— **some hairpins.** delle forcine.
    DAYL-lay fohr-CHEE-nay.

1432. —— **a hot-water bottle.**
    una bottiglia per l'acqua calda.
    *OO-nah boht-TEE-layh pyar LAHK-kwah
    KAHL-dah.*

1433. —— **an icebag.** una borsa da ghiaccio.
    OO-nah BOHR-sah dah GYAHCH-chyoh.

1434. —— **some insect repellent.**
della lozione contro gli insetti.
DAYL-lah lo-TSYOH-nay KOHN-tro lyee een-SET-tee.

1435. —— **some iodine.** della tintura di iodio.
DAYL-lah teen-TOO-rah dee YAW-dyoh.

1436. —— **a laxative (mild).** un lassativo (leggero).
oon lahs-sah-TEE-vo (lej-JAYR-ro).

1437. —— **a lipstick.** del rossetto per le labbra.
dayl rohs-SET-toh payr lay LAHB-brah.

1438. —— **a medicine dropper.** un contagocce.
oon kohn-tah-GOHCH-chay.

1439. —— **a mouthwash.**
qualcosa per risciacquarsi la bocca.
kwahl-KAW-sah payr ree-shyahk-KWAHR-see lah BOHK-kah.

1440. —— **a nail file.** una limetta da unghie.
OO-nah lee-MAYT-tah dah OON-gyay.

1441. —— **some nail polish.**
dello smalto per le unghie.
DAYL-lo SMAHL-toh payr lay OON-gyay.

1442. —— **some nail polish remover.**
qualcosa per togliere lo smalto dalle unghie.
kwahl-KAW-sah payr TAW-lyay-ray lo SMAHL-toh DAHL-lay OON-gyay.

1443. —— **some hydrogen peroxide.**
dell'acqua ossigenata.
dayl-LAHK-kwah ohs-see-jay-NAH-tah.

1444. —— **some powder.** della cipria.
DAYL-lah CHEE-pryah.

1445. —— **some talcum powder.** del talco.
dayl TAHL-ko.

1446. —— **a razor.**   un rasoio.   *oon rah-SO-yoh.*

1447. —— **a package of razor blades.**
un pacchetto di lamette.
oon pahk-KAYT-toh dee lah-MET-tay.

1448. —— **some rouge.**   del rossetto per la faccia.
dayl rohs-SET-toh payr lah FAHCH-chyah.

1449. —— **some safety pins.**
degli spilli di sicurezza.
DAY-lyee SPEEL-lee dee see-koo-RAYTS-sah.

1450. —— **some sanitary napkins.**
degli assorbenti igienici.
DAY-lyee ahs-sohr-BEN-tee ee-JYEH-nee-chee.

1451. —— **a sedative.**   un calmante.
oon kahl-MAHN-tay.

1452. —— **some shampoo.**   dello shampoo.
DAYL-lo "shampoo."

1453. —— **some shaving cream (brushless).**
della crema da barba (senza pennello).
DAYL-lah KREH-mah dah BAHR-bah (SEN-tsah payn-NEL-lo).

1454. —— **some shaving lotion.**
della lozione per la barba.
DAYL-lah lo-TSYOH-nay payr lah BAHR-bah.

1455. —— **some smelling salts.**
dei sali d'ammoniaca.
day SAH-lee dahm-mo-NEE-ah-kah.

1456. —— **a bar of soap.**   un pezzo di sapone.
oon PET-tso dee sah-PO-nay.

1457. —— **some soap flakes.**
del sapone in polvere.
dayl sah-PO-nay een POHL-vay-ray.

1458. —— **a pair of sunglasses.**
un paio di occhiali da sole.
oon PAH-yoh dee okh-KYAH-lee dah SO-lay.

1459. —— **some sunburn ointment.**
una pomata per le bruciature del sole.
OO-nah po-MAH-tah payr lay broo-chyah-
TOO-ray dayl SO-lay.

1460. —— **some suntan oil.**
della crema per abbronzare.
DAYL-lah KREH-mah payr ahb-brohn-DZAH-
ray.

1461. —— **a thermometer.**   un termometro.
oon tayr-MAW-may-tro.

1462. —— **a toothbrush.**   uno spazzolino da denti.
OO-no spaht-tso-LEE-no dah DEN-tee.

1463. —— **a tube of toothpaste.**
un tubetto di pasta dentifricia.
oon too-BAYT-toh dee PAH-stah dayn-tee-
FREE-chyah.

1464. —— **a can of toothpowder.**
una scatola di polvere dentifricia.
OO-nah SKAH-toh-lah dee POHL-vay-ray
dayn-tee-FREE-chyah.

CLOTHING STORE
VESTIARIO

1465. I want to buy [a bathing cap].
Vorrei comprare [una cuffia da bagno].
vohr-REH_ee kohm-PRAH-ray [OO-nah KOOF-fyah
dah BAH-nyoh].

1466. —— **a bathing suit.** un costume da bagno.
oon ko-STOO-may dah BAH-nyoh.

1467. —— **a blouse.** una camicetta.
OO-nah kah-mee-CHAYT-tah.

1468. —— **a brassière.** un reggipetto.
oon rayj-jee-PET-toh.

1469. —— **a coat.** un soprabito.
oon so-PRAH-bee-toh.

1470. —— **a collar.** un colletto.
oon kohl-LAYT-toh.

1471. —— **some diapers.**
dei pannolini da bambini.
day pahn-no-LEE-nee dah bahm-BEE-nee.

1472. —— **a dress.** un vestito.
oon vay-STEE-toh.

1473. —— **some children's dresses.**
dei vestiti per bambini.
day vay-STEE-tee payr bahm-BEE-nee.

1474. —— **a pair of garters.** un paio di giarettiere.
oon PAH-yoh dee jah-rayt-TYEH-ray.

1475. —— **a girdle.** un busto. *oon BOO-sto.*

1476. —— **a pair of gloves.** un paio di guanti.
oon PAH-yoh dee GWAHN-tee.

1477. —— **a handbag.** una borsetta.
OO-nah bohr-SAYT-tah.

1478. —— **a few handkerchiefs.**
alcuni fazzoletti.
ahl-KOO-nee faht-tso-LAYT-tee.

1479. —— **a hat.** un cappello. *oon kahp-PEL-lo.*

1480. —— **a fur jacket.** una giacca di pelliccia.
OO-nah JAHK-kah dee payl-LEECH-chyah.

1481. —— **some lingerie.** della biancheria.
DAYL-lah byahn-kay-REE-ah.

1482. —— **some neckties.** delle cravatte.
DAYL-lay krah-VAHT-tay.

1483. —— **a nightgown.**
una camicia da notte.
OO-nah kah-MEE-chyah dah NAWT-tay.

1484. —— **a pair of panties.**
un paio di mutandine.
oon PAH-yoh dee moo-tahn-DEE-nay.

1485. —— **a pair of pajamas.** un paio di pigiama.
oon PAH-yoh dee pee-JYAH-mah.

1486. —— **a petticoat.** una sottoveste.
OO-nah soht-toh-VEH-stay.

1487. —— **a raincoat.** un impermeabile.
oon eem-payr-may-AH-bee-lay.

1488. —— **a robe.** una vestaglia.
OO-nah vay-STAH-lyah.

1489. —— **a scarf.** uno scialle.
OO-no SHYAHL-lay.

1490. —— **a pair of shoes.** un paio di scarpe.
oon PAH-yoh dee SKAHR-pay.

1491. —— **a pair of shoelaces.** un paio di lacci.
oon PAH-yoh dee LAHCH-chee.

1492. —— **a pair of shorts.** un paio di mutande.
oon PAH-yoh dee moo-TAHN-day.

1493. —— **a skirt.** una gonna.
OO-nah GAWN-nah.

1494. —— **a slip.** una sottana.
OO-nah soht-TAH-nah.

1495. —— **a pair of slippers.**
un paio di pantofole.
oon PAH-yoh dee pahn-TAW-fo-lay.

1496. —— **a half-dozen pairs of socks.**
mezza dozzina di calzini.
MEHD-dzah dohd-DZEE-nah dee kahl-TSEE-nee.

1497. —— **a pair of nylon stockings.**
un paio di calze di nailon.
oon PAH-yoh dee KAHL-tsay dee "nylon."

1498. —— **a suit.** un tailleur.   *oon tah-YEHR.*

1499. —— **a pair of suspenders.**
un paio di bretelle.
oon PAH-yoh dee bray-TEL-lay.

1500. —— **a sweater.** un golf.   *oon gohlf.*

1501. —— **a pair of trousers.**   un paio di calzoni.
oon PAH-yoh dee kahl-TSO-nee.

1502. —— **some underwear.**
della biancheria personale.
DAYL-lah byahn-kay-REE-ah payr-so-NAH-lay.

BOOKSHOP AND STATIONER
LIBRERIA E CARTOLERIA

1503. **Where is there [a bookshop]?**
Dov'è [una libreria]?
doh-VEH [OO-nah lee-bray-REE-ah]?

1504. —— **a stationer.**
una cartoleria.
OO-nah kahr-toh-lay-REE-ah.

1505. —— a news dealer.
un giornalaio.
oon johr-nah-LAH-yoh.

1506. I want to buy [a book].
Vorrei comprare [un libro].
vohr-REH_ee kohm-PRAH-ray [oon LEE-bro].

1507. —— a guidebook.
una guida.
OO-nah GWEE-dah.

1508. —— a blotter.
una carta sugante.
OO-nah KAHR-tah soo-GAHN-tay.

1509. —— an assortment of picture postcards.
delle cartoline illustrate assortite.
DAYL-lay kahr-toh-LEE-nay eel-loo-STRAH-tay ahs-sohr-TEE-tay.

1510. —— a deck of playing cards.
un mazzo di carte da gioco.
oon MAHT-tso dee KAHR-tay dah JYAW-ko.

1511. —— an English-Italian dictionary.
un dizionario inglese-italiano.
oon dee-tsyoh-NAH-ryoh een-GLAY-say-ee-tah-LYAH-no.

1512. —— one dozen envelopes.
una dozzina di buste.
OO-nah dohd-DZEE-nah dee BOO-stay.

1513. —— an eraser.
una gomma.
OO-nah GOHM-mah.

1514. —— some ink.
dell'inchiostro.
dayl-leen-KYAW-stro.

1515. —— **some magazines.**
delle riviste.
DAYL-lay ree-VEE-stay.

1516. —— **a map of ——.**
una carta geografica di ——.
OO-nah KAHR-tah jay-o-GRAH-fee-kah dee
—— .

1517. —— **some artist's materials.**
degli articoli per pittori.
DAY-lyee ahr-TEE-ko-lee payr peet-TOH-ree.

1518. —— **a newspaper.**
un giornale.
oon johr-NAH-lay.

1519. —— **some carbon paper.**
della carta carbone.
DAYL-lah KAHR-tah kahr-BO-nay.

1520. —— **some tissue paper.**
della carta velina.
DAYL-lah KAHR-tah vay-LEE-nah.

1521. —— **a sheet of wrapping paper.**
un foglio di carta da imballaggio.
*oon FAW-lyoh dee KAHR-tah dah eem-bahl-
LAHJ-jo.*

1522. —— **some writing paper.**
della carta da scrivere.
DAYL-lah KAHR-tah dah SKREE-vay-ray.

1523. —— **a ream of typewriting paper.**
una risma di carta per macchina da scrivere.
*OO-nah REE-zmah dee KAHR-tah payr
MAHK-kee-nah dah SKREE-vay-ray.*

1524. —— **a typewriter ribbon.**
un nastro per la macchina da scrivere.
oon NAH-stro payr lah MAHK-kee-nah dah SKREE-vay-ray.

1525. —— **a fountain pen.**
una penna stilografica.
OO-nah PAYN-nah stee-lo-GRAH-fee-kah.

1526. —— **a pencil.**
una matita.
OO-nah mah-TEE-tah.

1527. —— **some string.**
dello spago.
DAYL-lo SPAH-go.

1528. —— **a roll of Scotch tape.**
un rotolino di carta gommata.
oon ro-toh-LEE-no dee KAHR-tah gohm-MAH-tah.

PHOTOGRAPHY

ARTICOLI FOTOGRAFICI

1529. I want a roll of movie film for this camera.
Vorrei un rotolino di pellicole cinematografiche per questa macchina.
vor-REH_ee oon ro-toh-LEE-no dee pel-LEE-ko-lay chee-nay-mah-toh-GRAH-fee-kay payr KWAY-stah MAHK-kee-nah.

1530. Do you sell [color film] flashbulbs?
Vendono [pellicole a colori] lampadine al magnesio?
VAYN-doh-no [pel-LEE-ko-lay-ah ko-LO-ree] lahm-pah-DEE-nay ahl mah-NYEH-zyoh?

1531. The size is ——.
La misura è ——.
lah mee-ZOO-rah eh ——.

1532. What is the charge for [developing a roll]?
Quanto costa [lo sviluppo di un rotolino]?
KWAHN-toh KAW-stah [lo svee-LOOP-po dee oon ro-toh-LEE-no]?

1533. —— an enlargement.
un ingrandimento.'
oon een-grahn-dee-MAYN-toh.

1534. —— for one print of each.
una copia di ognuna.
OO-nah KAW-pyah dee o-NYOO-nah.

1535. Please have this ready for me as soon as possible.
Per favore me lo faccia avere al più presto possibile.
payr fah-VO-ray may lo FAHCH-chyah ah-VAY-ray ahl pyoo PREH-sto pohs-SEE-bee-lay.

1536. May I take [a snapshot] some movies of you?
Posso farle [un'istantanea] un provino per il cinema?
PAWS-so FAHR-lay [oo-nee-stahn-TAH-nay-ah] oon pro-VEE-no payr eel CHEE-nay-mah?

BARBER SHOP AND BEAUTY PARLOR

BARBIERE E SALONE DI BELLEZZA

1537. Where is there [a good barber]?
Dov'è [un buon barbiere]?
doh-VEH [oon bwawn bahr-BYEH-ray]?

1538. —— **a beauty parlor.**
un salone di bellezza.
oon sah-LO-nay dee bayl-LAYT-tsah.

1539. I want to have [a haircut].
Vorrei farmi [tagliare i capelli].
vohr-REH_ee FAHR-mee [tah-LYAH-ray ee kah-PAYL-lee].

1540. —— **a facial.**
fare un massaggio della faccia.
FAH-ray oon mahs-SAHJ-jo DAYL-lah FAHCH-chyah.

1541. —— **a massage.**
fare un massaggio.
FAH-ray oon mahs-SAHJ-jo.

1542. —— **a hair set.**
mettere in piega i capelli.
MAYT-tay-ray een PYEH-gah ee kah-PAYL-lee.

1543. —— **a hair tint.**
tingere i capelli.
TEEN-jay-ray ee kah-PAYL-lee.

1544. —— **a manicure.**
fare le unghie.
FAH-ray lay OON-gyay.

1545. —— **a permanent wave.**
fare un'ondulazione permanente.
FAH-ray oo-nohn-doo-lah-TSYOH-nay payr-mah-NEN-tay.

1546. —— **a shoe shine.**
lucidare le scarpe.
loo-chee-DAH-ray lay SKAHR-pay.

1547. Can you do it now?
Lo può fare ora?
lo pwaw FAH-ray O-rah?

1548. Can I make an appointment for tomorrow?
Potrei fare un appuntamento per domani?
po-TREH_ee FAH-ray oon ahp-poon-tah-MAYN-toh payr doh-MAH-nee?

1549. I part my hair [on this side].
Porto la riga [da questa parte].
PAWR-toh lah REE-gah [dah KWAY-stah PAHR-tay].

1550. —— on the other side.
dall'altra parte.
dahl-LAHL-trah PAHR-tay.

1551. —— in the center.
al centro.
ahl CHEN-tro.

1552. Do not cut it at the top.
Non me li tagli sopra.
nawn may lee TAH-lyee SO-prah.

1553. Not too short.
Non troppo corti.
nawn TRAWP-po KOHR-tee.

1554. Thin it a little.
Li sfoltisca un po'.
lee sfohl-TEE-skah oon paw.

1555. (Do not) put on hair tonic.
(Non) metta del tonico.
(nawn) MAYT-tah dayl TAW-nee-ko.

LAUNDRY AND DRY CLEANING

LAVANDERIA E PULITURA A SECCO

1556. Does [this laundry] give one-day service?

Fanno servizio in giornata in [questa lavanderia]?

FAHN-no sayr-VEE-tsyoh een johr-NAH-tah een [KWAY-stah lah-vahn-day-REE-ah]?

1557. —— this dry cleaner.

questa tintoria.

KWAY-stah teen-toh-REE-ah.

1558. Can I have some laundry done?

Posso far lavare della biancheria?

PAWS-so fahr lah-VAH-ray DAYL-lah byahn-kay-REE-ah?

1559. Please wash and mend this shirt.

Per favore lavi e rammendi questa camicia.

payr fah-VO-ray LAH-vee ay rahm-MEN-dee KWAY-stah kah-MEE-chyah.

1560. Do not wash this in hot water.

Questo non lo lavi con acqua calda.

KWAY-sto nawn lo LAH-vee kohn AHK-kwah KAHL-dah.

1561. Use lukewarm water.

Usi dell'acqua tiepida.

OO-zee dayl-LAHK-kwah TYEH-pee-dah.

1562. Remove this stain.

Tolga questa macchia.

TAWL-gah KWAY-stah MAHK-kyah.

1563. (Do not) starch the collar.

(Non) inamidi il colletto.

(nawn) ee-NAH-mee-dee eel kohl-LAYT-toh.

1564. I want this suit cleaned and pressed.
    Voglio far pulire e stirare quest'abito.
    VAW-lyoh fahr poo-LEE-ray ay stee-RAH-ray kway-
       STAH-bee-toh.

1565. The pocket is torn.
    La tasca è strappata.
    lah TAH-skah eh strahp-PAH-tah.

1566. The belt is missing.
    Manca la cintura.
    MAHN-kah lah cheen-TOO-rah.

1567. Will you sew on the buttons?
    Mi può attaccare i bottoni?
    mee pwaw aht-tahk-KAH-ray ee boht-TOH-nee?

1568. Replace the zipper.
    Cambi la chiusura lampo.
    KAHM-bee lah kyoo-SOO-rah LAHM-po.

REPAIRS
RIPARAZIONI

1569. My glasses were broken.
    Mi si sono rotti gli occhiali.
    mee see SO-no ROHT-tee lyee ohk-KYAH-lee.

1570. Where can they be repaired?
    Dove li posso far riparare?
    DOH-vay lee PAWS-so fahr ree-pah-RAH-ray?

1571. Please regulate my watch.
    Per favore, mi regoli l'orologio.
    payr fah-VO-ray, mee REH-go-lee lo-ro-LAW-jo.

1572. My clock [loses] gains time.
    Il mio orologio [va indietro] va avanti.
    eel MEE-o o-ro-LAW-jo [vah een-DYAY-tro] vah
       ah-VAHN-tee.

1573. My hearing aid needs adjustment.
Il mio apparecchio acustico deve essere regolato.
*eel MEE-o ahp-pah-RAYK-kyoh ah-KOO-stee-ko
DAY-vay ES-say-ray ray-go-LAH-toh.*

1574. Repair [the sole].
Ripari [la suola].
ree-PAH-ree [lah SWAW-lah].

1575. —— the heel.
il tacco.
eel TAHK-ko.

1576. —— the uppers.
la parte di sopra.
lah PAHR-tay dee SO-prah.

1577. —— the strap.
la cinghia.
lah CHEEN-gyah.

HEALTH AND ILLNESS
SALUTE E MALATTIE

1578. I wish to have [a doctor].
Vorrei avere [un medico].
vohr-REH ee ah-VAY-ray [oon MEH-dee-ko].

1579. —— an American doctor.
un medico americano.
oon MEH-dee-ko ah-may-ree-KAH-no.

1580. —— a doctor who speaks English.
un medico che parla l'inglese.
oon MEH-dee-ko kay PAHR-lah leen-GLAY-say.

1581. —— a specialist. uno specialista.
OO-no spay-chyah-LEE-stah.

1582. —— **a chiropodist.**   un pedicure.
      oon pay-dee-KOO-ray.

1583. —— **an optometrist.**   un oculista.
      oon o-koo-LEE-stah.

1584. **Is the doctor in?**   C'è il dottore?
      cheh eel doht-TOH-ray?

1585. **I have something in my eye.**
      Ho qualche cosa nell'occhio.
      aw KWAHL-kay KAW-sah nayl-LAWK-kyoh.

1586. **I have a headache.**   Ho mal di testa.
      aw mahl dee TAY-stah.

1587. **I have a pain in my back.**
      Ho un dolore nella schiena.
      aw oon doh-LO-ray NAYL-lah SKYEH-nah.

1588. **I do not sleep well.**   Non dormo bene.
      nawn DAWR-mo BEH-nay.

1589. **Can you give me something to relieve my
     allergy?**
      Mi può dare qualche cosa per darmi sollievo
      dall'allergia?
      *mee pwaw DAH-ray KWAHL-kay KAW-sah payr
      DAHR-mee sohl-LYEH-vo dahl-lahl-layr-JEE-
      ah?*

1590. **An appendicitis attack.**
      Un attacco d'appendicite.
      oon aht-TAHK-ko dahp-payn-dee-CHEE-tay.

1591. **An insect bite.**   Una puntura d'insetto.
      OO-nah poon-TOO-rah deen-SET-toh.

1592. **A blister.**   Una bollicina.
      OO-nah bohl-lee-CHEE-nah.

1593. A boil. Un foruncolo. *oon fo-ROON-ko-lo.*

1594. A burn. Una scottatura.
OO-nah skoht-tah-TOO-rah.

1595. Chills. Brividi. *BREE-vee-dee.*

1596. A cold. Un raffreddore.
oon rahf-frayd-DOH-ray.

1597. Constipation. Stitichezza.
stee-tee-KAYT-tsah.

1598. A cough. La tosse. *lay TOHS-say.*

1599. A cramp. Un crampo. *oon KRAHM-po.*

1600. Diarrhoea. Diarrea. *dee-ahr-REH-ah.*

1601. Dysentery. Dissenteria.
dees-sayn-tay-REE-ah.

1602. An earache. Un mal d'orecchi.
oon mahl doh-RAYK-kee.

1603. A fever. La febbre. *lah FEB-bray.*

1604. Hay fever. Febbre del fieno.
FEB-bray dayl FYEH-no.

1605. Hoarseness. Raucedine.
rah_oo-CHEH-dee-nay.

1606. Indigestion. Indigestione.
een-dee-jay-STYOH-nay.

1607. Nausea. Nausea. *NAH_oo-zay-ah.*

1608. Pneumonia. Polmonite.
pohl-mo-NEE-tay.

1609. A sore throat. Un mal di gola.
oon mahl dee GO-lah.

1610. A sunburn. Una bruciatura dal sole.
OO-nah broo-chyah-TOO-rah dahl SO-lay.

1611. A virus. Un virus. *oon VEE-roos.*

1612. An infection. Un'infezione.
oo-neen-fay-TSYOH-nay.

1613. What shall I do? Che cosa devo fare?
kay KAW-sah DAY-vo FAH-ray?

1614. Do I have to go to a hospital?
Devo andare all'ospedale?
DAY-vo ahn-DAH-ray ahl-lo-spay-DAH-lay?

1615. Must I stay in bed? Devo restare a letto?
DAY-vo ray-STAH-ray ah LET-toh?

1616. Is it contagious? È contagioso?
eh kohn-tah-JO-so?

1617. I feel [better] worse.
Mi sento [meglio] peggio.
mee SEN-toh [MEH-lyoh] PEJ-jo.

1618. Can I travel on Monday?
Potrò viaggiare lunedì?
po-TRAW vyahj-JAH-ray loo-nay-DEE?

1619. When will you come again?
Quando ritornerà?
KWAHN-doh ree-tohr-nay-RAH?

1620. When shall I take [the medicine]?
Quando devo prendere [la medicina]?
*KWAHN-doh DAY-vo PREN-day-ray [lah may-
dee-CHEE-nah]?*

1621. —— the pills. le pillole. *lay PEEL-lo-lay.*

1622. The prescription. La ricetta.
lah ree-CHET-tah.

1623. Every hour. Ogni ora. *O-nyee O-rah.*

1624. [Before] after meals. [Prima] dopo i pasti.
[PREE-mah] DOH-po ee PAH-stee.

1625. On going to bed. Prima di andare a letto.
PREE-mah dee ahn-DAH-ray ah LET-toh.

1626. On getting up. Appena alzato.
ahp-PAY-nah ahl-TSAH-toh.

1627. Twice a day. Due volte al giorno.
DOO-ay VAWL-tay ahl JOHR-no.

1628. A drop. Una goccia.
OO-nah GOHCH-chyah.

1629. A teaspoonful. Un cucchiaino.
oon kook-kyah-EE-no.

1630. X-rays. Raggi x. *RAHJ-jee eeks.*

ACCIDENTS

DISGRAZIE

1631. There has been an accident.
C'è stata una disgrazia.
cheh STAH-tah OO-nah dee-ZGRAH-tsyah.

1632. Please get [a doctor].
Per favore faccia venire [un medico].
payr fah-VO-ray FAHCH-chyah vay-NEE-ray [oon MEH-dee-ko].

1633. —— a nurse. un'infermiera.
oo-neen-fayr-MYEH-rah.

1634. —— an ambulance. un'ambulanza.
oo-nahm-boo-LAHN-tsah.

1635. He has [fallen] fainted. È [caduto] svenuto.
eh [kah-DOO-toh] zvay-NOO-toh.

1636. She has [a bruise]. Ha [un livido].
ah [oon LEE-vee-doh].

1637. —— **a cut.**   un taglio.   *oon TAH-lyoh.*

1638. —— **a fracture.**   una frattura.
OO-nah fraht-TOO-rah.

1639. —— **a sprain.**   una slogatura.
OO-nah zlo-gah-TOO-rah.

1640. Can you dress this wound?
Può medicare questa ferita?
pwaw may-dee-KAH-ray KWAY-stah fay-REE-tah?

1641. It is bleeding.   Sanguina.   *SAHN-gwee-nah.*

1642. It is swollen.   È gonfio.   *eh GOHN-fyoh.*

1643. I need something for a tourniquet.
Mi ci vuole qualcosa per fare una legatura
stretta.
*mee chee VWAW-lay kwahl-KAW-sah payr FAH-ray
OO-nah lay-gah-TOO-rah STRAYT-tah.*

1644. Are you all right?   Non le è successo niente?
nawn lay eh sooch-CHES-so NYEN-tay?

1645. I have hurt my foot.
Mi son fatto male al piede.
mee sohn FAHT-toh MAH-lay ahl PYEH-day.

1646. I want to rest a moment.
Voglio riposare un momento.
VAW-lyoh ree-po-SAH-ray oon mo-MAYN-toh.

1647. Please notify [my husband].
Per favore informi [mio marito].
*payr fah-VO-ray een-FOHR-mee [MEE-o mah-REE-
toh].*

1648. —— **my wife.**   mia moglie.
MEE-ah MO-lyay.

1649. —— **my friend.**   il mio amico.
eel MEE-o ah-MEE-ko.

PARTS OF THE BODY
PARTI DEL CORPO UMANO

1650. The appendix. L'appendice.
lahp-payn-DEE-chay.

1651. The arm. Il braccio. *eel BRAHCH-chyoh.*

1652. The artery. L'arteria. *lahr-TEH-ryah.*

1653. The back. La schiena. *lah SKYEH-nah.*

1654. The blood. Il sangue. *eel SAHN-gway.*

1655. The blood vessels. I vasi sanguigni.
ee VA-zee sahn-GWEE-nyee.

1656. The bone. L'osso. *LAWS-so.*

1657. The brain. Il cervello. *eel chayr-VEL-lo.*

1658. The breast. Il petto. *eel PET-toh.*

1659. The cheek. La guancia.
lah GWAHN-chyah.

1660. The chest. Il petto. *eel PET-toh.*

1661. The chin. Il mento. *eel MAYN-toh.*

1662. The collarbone. L'osso del collo.
LAWS-so dayl KAWL-lo.

1663. The ear. L'orecchio. *lo-RAYK-kyoh.*

1664. The elbow. Il gomito. *eel GO-mee-toh.*

1665. The eye. L'occhio. *LAWK-kyoh.*

1666. The eyebrows. Le sopracciglia.
lay so-prahch-CHEE-lyah.

1667. The eyelashes. Le ciglia. *lay CHEE-lyah.*

1668. The eyelid. La palpebra. *lah PAHL-pay-brah.*

1669. The face. La faccia. *lah FAHCH-chyah.*

1670. The finger. Il dito. *eel DEE-toh.*

1671. The fingernail. L'unghia. *LOON-gyah.*

1672. The foot. Il piede. *eel PYEH-day.*

1673. The forehead. La fronte. *lah FROHN-tay.*

1674. The gall bladder. La cistifellea.
lah chee-stee-FEL-lay-ah.

1675. The glands. Le glandole.
lay GLAHN-doh-lay.

1676. The gums. Le gengive. *lay jayn-JEE-vay.*

1677. The hair. I capelli *ee kah-PAYL-lee.*

1678. The head. La testa. *lah TEH-stah.*

1679. The hand. La mano. *lah MAH-no.*

1680. The heart. Il cuore. *eel KWAW-ray.*

1681. The heel. Il calcagno. *eel kahl-KAH-nyoh.*

1682. The hip. L'anca. *LAHN-kah.*

1683. The intestines. L'intestino.
leen-tay-STEE-no.

1684. The jaw. La mascella.
lah mah-SHAYL-lah.

1685. The joint. L'articolazione.
lahr-tee-ko-lah-TSYOH-nay.

1686. The kidney. Il rene. *eel REH-nay.*

1687. The knee. Il ginocchio.
eel jee-NAWK-kyoh.

1688. The leg. La gamba. *lah GAHM-bah.*

1689. The lip. Il labbro. *eel LAHB-bro.*

1690. The liver. Il fegato. *eel FAY-gah-toh.*

1691. The lung. Il polmone. *eel pohl-MO-nay.*

1692. The mouth. La bocca. *lah BOHK-kah.*

1693. The muscle. Il muscolo. *eel MOO-sko-lo.*

1694. The neck. Il collo. *eel KAWL-lo.*

1695. The nerve. Il nervo. *eel NEHR-vo.*

1696. The nose. Il naso. *eel NAH-so.*

1697. The rib. La costola. *lah KAW-sto-lah.*

1698. The shoulder. La spalla. *lah SPAHL-lah.*

1699. The skin. La pelle. *lah PEL-lay.*

1700. The skull. Il cranio. *eel KRAH-nyoh.*

1701. The spine. La spina dorsale.
lah SPEE-nah dohr-SAH-lay.

1702. The stomach. Lo stomaco.
lo STAW-mah-ko.

1703. The teeth. I denti. *ee DEN-tee.*

1704. The toe. Il dito del piede.
eel DEE-toh dayl PYEH-day.

1705. The toenail. L'unghia del piede.
LOON-gyah dayl PYEH-day.

1706. The tongue. La lingua. *lah LEEN-gwah.*

1707. The tonsils. Le tonsille. *lay tohn-SEEL-lay.*

1708. The vein. La vena. *lah VAY-nah.*

1709. The wrist. Il polso. *eel POHL-so.*

DENTIST

IL DENTISTA

1710. Do you know a good dentist?
Conosce un buon dentista?
ko-NO-shay oon bwawn dayn-TEE-stah?

1711. This wisdom tooth hurts.
Questo dente del giudizio mi fa male.
KWAY-sto DEN-tay dayl joo-DEE-tsyoh mee fah MAH-lay.

1712. I have lost a filling.
Ho perduto un'impiombatura.
aw payr-DOO-toh oo-neem-pyohm-bah-TOO-rah.

1713. I think I have [an abscess].
Penso di avere [un ascesso a un dente].
PEN-so dee ah-VAY-ray [oon ah-SHEHS-so ah oon DEN-tay].

1714. —— a broken tooth.
un dente rotto.
oon DEN-tay ROHT-toh.

1715. Can you fix [the bridge] temporarily?
Mi può riparare [il ponte] provvisoriamente?
mee pwaw ree-pah-RAH-ray [eel POHN-tay] prohv-vee-zo-ryah-MAYN-tay?

1716. —— the denture.
la dentiera.
lah dayn-TYEH-rah.

1717. You are hurting me.
Mi sta facendo male.
mee stah fah-CHAYN-doh MAH-lay.

1718. Please give me [a local anesthetic].
Per favore mi faccia [un'anestesia locale].
payr fah-VO-ray mee FAHCH-chyah [oo-nah-nay-stay-ZEE-ah lo-KAH-lay].

1719. —— gas.
un'anestesia a gas.
oo-nah-nay-stay-ZEE-ah ah gahz.

USEFUL INFORMATION
INFORMAZIONI UTILI

1720. What time is it?
Che ora è?
kay O-rah eh?

I am in a hurry
Ho fretta

1721. It is [early].
È [presto].
eh [PREH-sto].

sono in Ritardo
I am late

1722. —— too late.
troppo tardi.
TRAWP-po TAHR-dee.

io sono in
anticipo
I am early

1723. It is [two o'clock] (A.M.).
Sono [le due].
SO-no [lay DOO-ay].

1724. —— two o'clock (P.M.).
le quattordici.
lay kwaht-TAWR-dee-chee.

1725. —— half-past three (P.M.).
le quindici e mezzo.
lay KWEEN-dee-chee ay MED-dzo.

1726. —— quarter-past four (P.M.).
le sedici e un quarto.
lay SAY-dee-chee ay oon KWAHR-toh.

1727. —— quarter to five (P.M.).
le diciassette meno un quarto.
lay dee-chyahs-SET-tay MAY-no oon KWAHR-toh.

1728. At ten minutes to six (P.M.).
Alle diciotto meno dieci.
AHL-lay dee-CHYAWT-toh MAY-no DYEH-chee.

1729. At twenty minutes past seven (P.M.).
Alle diciannove e venti.
AHL-lay dee-chyahn-NAW-vay ay VAYN-tee.

1730. In the morning.
La mattina.
lah maht-TEE-nah.

1731. In the afternoon.
Il pomeriggio.
eel po-may-REEJ-jo.

1732. In the evening.
La sera.
lah SAY-rah.

1733. At noon.
A mezzogiorno.
ah mayd-dzo-JOHR-no.

1734. The day.
Il giorno.   *i g i o r i*
eel JOHR-no.

1735. The night.
La notte.
lah NAWT-tay.

1736. Midnight.
Mezzanotte.
mayd-dzah-NAWT-tay.

1737. Last night.
Ieri sera.
YEH-ree SAY-rah.

1738. Yesterday.
Ieri.
YEH-ree.

1739. Today.
Oggi.
AWJ-jee.

1740. Tonight.
Stasera.
stah-SAY-rah.

1741. Tomorrow.
Domani.
doh-MAH-nee.

1742. Last month.
Il mese scorso.
eel MAY-say SKOHR-so.

1743. Last year.
L'anno scorso.
LAHN-no SKOHR-so.

1744. Next Sunday.
Domenica prossima.
doh-MAY-nee-kah PRAWS-see-mah.

1745. Next week.
La settimana prossima.
lah sayt-tee-MAH-nah PRAWS-see-mah.

1746. The day before yesterday.
L'altro ieri.
LAHL-tro YEH-ree.

1747. The day after tomorrow.
  Dopodomani.
  doh-po-doh-MAH-nee.

1748. Two weeks ago.
  Due settimane fa.
  DOO-ay sayt-tee-MAH-nay fah.

WEATHER

IL TEMPO

1749. How is the weather today?
  Che tempo fa oggi?
  kay TEM-po fah AWJ-jee?

1750. Is it [cold]?
  Fa [freddo]?
  fah [FRAYD-doh]?

1751. —— fair.
  bel tempo.
  bel TEM-po.

1752. —— hot.
  caldo.
  KAHL-doh.

1753. It is still raining.
  Piove ancora.
  PYAW-vay ahn-KO-rah.

1754. Is it snowing?
  Nevica?
  NAY-vee-kah?

1755. It is sunny.
  C'è sole.
  cheh SO-lay.

1756. It is very warm.
Fa molto caldo.
fah MOHL-toh KAHL-doh.

1757. I want to sit [in the shade].
Vorrei sedermi [all'ombra].
vohr-REH_ee say-DAYR-mee [ahl-LOHM-brah].

1758. —— in the sun.
al sole.
ahl SO-lay.

DAYS OF THE WEEK
I GIORNI DELLA SETTIMANA

1759. Monday.   Lunedì.   *loo-nay-DEE.*

1760. Tuesday.   Martedì.   *mahr-tay-DEE.*

1761. Wednesday.   Mercoledì.   *mayr-ko-lay-DEE.*

1762. Thursday.   Giovedì.   *jo-vay-DEE.*

1763. Friday.   Venerdì.   *vay-nayr-DEE.*

1764. Saturday.   Sabato.   *SAH-bah-toh.*

1765. Sunday.   Domenica.   *doh-MAY-nee-kah.*

MONTHS AND SEASONS
I MESI E LE STAGIONI

1766. January.   Gennaio.   *jayn-NAH-yoh.*

1767. February.   Febbraio.   *fayb-BRAH-yoh.*

1768 March.   Marzo.   *MAHR-tso.*

1769. April.   Aprile.   *ah-PREE-lay.*

1770. May. Maggio. *MAHJ-jo.*

1771. June. Giugno. *JOO-nyoh.*

1772. July. Luglio. *LOO-lyoh.*

1773. August. Agosto. *ah-GO-sto.*

1774. September. Settembre. *sayt-TEM-bray.*

1775. October. Ottobre. *oht-TOH-bray.*

1776. November. Novembre. *no-VEM-bray.*

1777. December. Dicembre. *dee-CHEM-bray.*

1778. Spring. Primavera. *pree-mah-VAY-rah.*

1779. Summer. Estate. *ay-STAH-tay.*

1780. Autumn. Autumno. *ah‿oo-TOON-no.*

1781. Winter. Inverno. *een-VEHR-no.*

HOLIDAYS AND GREETINGS
FESTE E AUGURI

1782. Christmas. Natale. *nah-TAH-lay.*

1783. Easter. Pasqua. *PAH-skwah.*

1784. Good Friday. Venerdì santo.
vay-nayr-DEE SAHN-toh.

1785. Lent. La quaresima.
lah kwah-RAY-zee-mah.

1786. New Year's. Capodanno.
kah-po-DAHN-no.

1787. A legal holiday. Un giorno festivo.
oon JOHR-no fay-STEE-vo.

1788. Happy Birthday. Buon compleanno.
bwawn kohm-play-AHN-no.

1789. Happy New Year. Buon Anno.
   bwawn AHN-no.

1790. Merry Christmas. Buon Natale.
   bwawn nah-TAH-lay.

NUMBERS
NUMERI

1791. One. Uno. *OO-no.*

Two. Due. *DOO-ay.*

Three. Tre. *tray.*

Four. Quattro. *KWAHT-tro.*

Five. Cinque. *CHEEN-kway.*

Six. Sei. *SEH_ee.*

Seven. Sette. *SET-tay.*

Eight. Otto. *AWT-toh.*

Nine. Nove. *NAW-vay.*

Ten. Dieci. *DYEH-chee.*

Eleven. Undici. *OON-dee-chee.*

Twelve. Dodici. *DOH-dee-chee.*

Thirteen. Tredici. *TRAY-dee-chee.*

Fourteen. Quattordici. *kwaht-TOHR-dee-chee.*

Fifteen. Quindici. *KWEEN-dee-chee.*

Sixteen. Sedici. *SAY-dee-chee.*

Seventeen. Diciassette.
dee-chyahs-SET-tay.

Eighteen. Diciotto. *dee-CHYAWT-toh.*

Nineteen. Diciannove.

dee-chyahn-NAW-vay..

Twenty. Venti. *VAYN-tee.*

Twenty-one. Ventuno. *vayn-TOO-no.*

Twenty-two. Ventidue. *vayn-tee-DOO-ay.*

Thirty. Trenta. *TRAYN-tah.*

Thirty-one. Trentuno. *trayn-TOO-no.*

Forty. Quaranta. *kwah-RAHN-tah.*

Fifty. Cinquanta. *cheen-KWAHN-tah.*

Sixty. Sessanta. *says-SAHN-tah.*

Seventy. Settanta. *sayt-TAHN-tah.*

Seventy-one. Settantuno. *sayt-tahn-TOO-no.*

Eighty. Ottanta. *oht-TAHN-tah.*

Eighty-one. Ottantuno. *oht-tahn-TOO-no.*

Ninety. Novanta. *no-VAHN-tah.*

Ninety-one. Novantuno.

no-vahn-TOO-no.

One hundred. Cento. *CHEN-toh.*

Two hundred. Due cento.

DOO-ay CHEN-toh.

One thousand. Mille. *MEEL-lay.*

Two thousand. Due mila.

DOO-ay MEE-lah.

Today's date is ——. Oggi è ——.

AWJ-jee eh ——.

NUMBERS: ORDINALS
NUMERI: ORDINALI

1792. First. Primo. *PREE-mo.*

Second. Secondo. *say-KOHN-doh.*

Third. Terzo. *TEHR-tso.*

Fourth. Quarto. *KWAHR-toh.*

Fifth. Quinto. *KWEEN-toh.*

Sixth. Sesto. *SEH-sto.*

Seventh. Settimo. *SET-tee-mo.*

Eighth. Ottavo. *oht-TAH-vo.*

Ninth. Nono. *NAW-no.*

Tenth. Decimo. *DEH-chee-mo.*

USEFUL ARTICLES
ARTICOLI VARI

1793. The ash tray. Il portacenere.
eel pohr-tah-CHAY-nay-ray.

1794. The basket. Il cestino. *eel chay-STEE-no.*

1795. The bobby pins. Le mollette.
lay mohl-LAYT-tay.

1796. The bottle opener. L'apribottiglie.
lah-pree-boht-TEE-lyay.

1797. The box. La scatola. *lah SKAH-toh-lah.*

1798. The bracelet. Il braccialetto.
eel brahch-chyah-LAYT-toh.

1799. The bulb (**light**). La lampadina.
lah lahm-pah-DEE-nah.

1800. The candy.   Le caramelle.
lay kah-rah-MEL-lay.

1801. The can opener.   L'apriscatole.
lah-pree-SKAH-toh-lay.

1802. The china.   Le stoviglie.   *lay sto-VEE-lyay.*

1803. The clock.   L'orologio.   *lo-ro-LAW-jo.*

1804. The cloth.   La stoffa.   *lah STAWF-fah.*

1805. The compact.   Il portacipria.
eel pohr-tah-CHEE-pryah.

1806. The cork.   Il turacciolo.
eel too-RAHCH-chyoh-lo.

1807. The corkscrew.   Il cavatappi.
eel kah-vah-TAHP-pee.

1808. The cotton.   Il cotone.   *eel ko-TOH-nay.*

1809. The cuff links.   I gemelli.   *ee jay-MEL-lee.*

1810. The cushion.   Il cuscino.   *eel koo-SHEE-ŋo.*

1811. The doll.   La bambola.   *lah BAHM-bo-lah.*

1812. The earrings.   Gli orecchini.
lyee o-rayk-KEE-nee.

1813. The embroidery.   Il ricamo.
eel ree-KAH-mo.

1814. The flashlight.   La lampadina portatile.
lah lahm-pah-DEE-nah pohr-TAH-tee-lay.

1815. The gum (chewing).
La gomma da masticare.
lah GOHM-mah dah mah-stee-KAH-ray.

1816. The hairnet.   La rete per i capelli.
lah RAY-tay payr ee kah-PAYL-lee.

1817. The handbag.   La borsetta.
lah bohr-SAYT-tah.

1818. The iron (flat).   Il ferro da stiro.
eel FAYR-ro dah STEE-ro.

1819. The jewelry (gold, silver).
I gioielli (d'oro, d'argento).
ee jyoh-YEL-lee (DAW-ro, dahr-JEN-toh).

1820. The lace.   Il pizzo.   *eel PEET-tso.*

1821. The leather.   Il cuoio.   *eel KWAW-yoh.*

1822. The linen.   Il lino.   *eel LEE-no.*

1823. The mirror.   Lo specchio.   *lo SPEK-kyoh*

1824. The music (sheet).   I fogli di musica.
ee FAW-lyee dee MOO-zee-kah.

1825. The musical instruments.
Gli strumenti musicali.
lyee stroo-MAYN-tee moo-zee-KAH-lee.

1826. The nail file.   La limetta da unghie.
lah lee-MAYT-tah dah OON-gyay.

1827. The necklace.   La collana.
lah kohl-LAH-nah.

1828. The needle.   L'ago.   *LAH-go.*

1829. The mosquito net.   La zanzariera.
lah dzahn-dzah-RYEH-rah.

1830. The notebook.   Il quaderno.
eel kwah-DEHR-no.

1831. The oil painting.   La pittura a olio.
lah peet-TOO-rah ah AW-lyoh.

1832. The pail.   Il secchio.   *eel SAYK-kyoh.*

1833. The penknife. Il temperino.
eel taym-pay-REE-no.

1834. The perfume. Il profumo. *eel pro-FOO-mo.*

1835. The pin. La spilla. *lah SPEEL-lah.*

1836. The radio. La radio. *lah RAH-dyoh.*

1837. The records (discs). I dischi. *ee DEE-skee.*

1838. The ring. L'anello. *lah-NEL-lo.*

1839. The rubbers. Le soprascarpe.
lay so-prah-SKAHR-pay.

1840. The rug. Il tappeto. *eel tahp-PAY-toh.*

1841. The safety pin. La spilla di sicurezza.
lah SPEEL-lah dee see-koo-RAYT-tsah.

1842. The scissors. Le forbici.
lay FAWR-bee-chee.

1843. The screw. La vite. *lah VEE-tay.*

1844. The silk. La seta. *lah SAY-tah.*

1845. The silver plate. L'argenteria.
lahr-jayn-tay-REE-ah.

1846. The stone (precious). La pietra (preziosa).
lah PYEH-trah (pray-TSYOH-sah).

1847. The stopper. Il tappo. *eel TAHP-po.*

1848. The straw. La paglia. *lah PAH-lyah.*

1849. The tablecloth. La tovaglia.
lah toh-VAH-lyah.

1850. The thimble. Il ditale. *eel dee-TAH-lay.*

1851. The thread. Il filo. *eel FEE-lo.*

1852. The toys. I giocattoli.
ee jo-KAHT-toh-lee.

1853. The umbrella.   L'ombrello.   *lohm-BREL-lo.*

1854. The vase.   Il vaso.   *eel VAH-zo.*

1855. The whiskbroom.   La spazzola.
lah SPAHT-tso-lah.

1856. The wire.   Il filo di ferro.
eel FEE-lo dee FEHR-ro.

1857. The wood.   Il legno.   *eel LAY-nyoh.*

1858. The wool.   La lana.   *lah LAH-nah.*

INDEX

All the sentences, phrases and words in this book are numbered consecutively from 1 to 1858. Numbers in the index refer you to each specific entry. In addition each major section (capitalized) is indexed according to page number in **bold** face. Parts of speech are indicated by the following italic abbreviations: *n.* for noun, *v.* for verb, *adj.* for adjective, *adv.* for adverb, *pron.* for pronoun, *prep.* for preposition.

MONEY CONVERTER AND TIPPING GUIDE FOR EUROPEAN TRAVEL

by Charles Vomacka

Covering every country in Free Europe (plus Egypt, Israel, Turkey, Russia, Poland, Czechoslovakia, and Rumania), this is the most complete guide of its type available today! 2 tables for each country convert U.S. money to foreign, foreign to dollars. You are told how much money is allowed in and out of each country, when you profit by changing cash here, when overseas. It answers just about every currency question you'll have.

All about tips, too. Travel agents say unwise tipping can be the most costly waste—can cut short your trip! Learn where hotels add a service charge, how much to give ship personnel, what to tip behind the Iron Curtain, and much more, about waiters, taxis, barbers, ushers, porters, restaurants, etc.

The guide includes special information for students, packing checklists, how many cigarettes are allowed into countries, bi-lingual agencies in each country, metric conversion and tire pressure tables, and still more information. It makes the perfect bon voyage gift.

PERPETUALLY REVISED! Unique—no other guide does this! Every change is picked up, saving you time and money. Plus other features you get nowhere else: monthly weather tables, European clothing sizes, and phone rates from all of Europe to the U.S. Do not confuse this with advertising gimmicks or giveaway "toys"—this is a serious compilation of accurate information, now 7 years in print.

128pp. 3½ x 5¼ .   20260-7   Paperbound **95¢**

NEW RUSSIAN-ENGLISH AND ENGLISH-RUSSIAN DICTIONARY

by M. A. O'Brien

This thoroughly tested reference work provides an unusually comprehensive guide to the reading, speaking and writing of Russian for both beginning and advanced students. Over 70,000 entries are provided, with full information on accentuation and grammatical classifications. All important meanings are given under each word, with many idiomatic uses and colloquialisms. Irregular verbs are listed in tables, while individual entries indicate stems, transitiveness, perfective and imperfective aspects, conjugation, and both regular and irregular sound changes. Genders, sound changes, irregularities, plurals are indicated for nouns, while irregular adjectives are given in both positive and comparative forms. Prepositional entries indicate cases governed. This is one of the very few dictionaries where accent changes within the conjugation of verbs and the declension of nouns are fully indicated.

Other features include pronunciation, translations of first names and geographical terms. A conversion table analyzes older Russian non-metric weights and measurements, while a bibliography lists more specialized language aids.

Complete unabridged reproduction. 738pp. 4½ x 6⅜.

20208-9   Paperbound **$2.75**

GERMAN—HOW TO SPEAK AND WRITE IT

by Joseph Rosenberg

This is probably the most delightful, useful and comprehensive elementary book available for learning spoken German, with or without a teacher. Working on the principle that a person learns more quickly by example than by rule, the author has put together a book that abounds in immediately usable German sentences and phrases on a wide variety of subjects.

This book, though eminently useful for classroom use, is especially useful for self study. The variety of teaching aids that this book places at your disposal is remarkable. The lessons contain dialogues, grammar and idiom studies (replete with examples), and extensive practice exercises. In addition there are 28 full-page and double-page sketches of specific scenes (a zoo, a theatre, etc.) with pertinent items numbered and identified in German and English; sketches and photographs which the student is asked to describe in German; German proverbs, jokes, etc.

The dialogues and reading material encompass an exceptionally wide range of real-life situations, and are extended to include most of the basic vocabulary one would need in each situation. The analysis of German pronunciation is very comprehensive. The practice exercises are carefully designed to allow the student to use what he has learned. The closing sections contain a summary of grammar, and a valuable guide to German literature.

Index. 600 illustrations. 384pp. 5⅜ x 8½.

20271-2 Paperbound **$2.50**

ESSENTIAL ENGLISH GRAMMAR
by Philip Gucker

Written by a highly gifted teacher who has specialized in adult education, this basic English grammar has been designed for adults with limited learning time. It explains important points of grammar needed for everyday speech and comprehension, avoiding seldom-used forms that you are not likely to need. Anticipating your questions and enabling you to avoid misunderstandings, Mr. Gucker proceeds in easy, natural steps from the simple sentence through the various parts of speech to more difficult constructions. All terms are defined and all forms used are amply illustrated with model sentences and phrases. More than 600 practice exercises and solutions help to make this an excellent home-study text. Serving effectively as a supplement to a phrase or record course, as a crystal-clear course for students and teachers, Mr. Gucker's text provides a firm foundation in basic English grammar, whether English is your native tongue or a second language. Index.   x + 177pp. 5⅜ x 8.

21649-7   Paperbound **$1.25**

AN ENGLISH-FRENCH-GERMAN-SPANISH WORD FREQUENCY DICTIONARY

by Helen S. Eaton

Prepared under the auspices of the Committee on Modern Languages of the American Council on Education, this is a semantic frequency list of the 6,000 most frequently used words for each of four languages: English, French, German, and Spanish. It differs from ordinary word frequency lists in being based on concepts rather than words, so that you will not be misled by submeanings, synonyms, or variants. More than 200 pages of separate indexes enable you to locate individual words for each language; exact frequencies are indicated.

This indispensable book has long been recognized as a first-rate aid for anyone who is teaching or seriously studying a foreign language, since it indicates, as no other dictionary does, the importance of each word in each language. You need not waste time learning words you are not likely to use. Its ratings may be applied to other languages as well.

"A notable service, I commend it," E. Thorndike, Teachers College, Columbia University. xx + 442pp. 6⅛ x 9¼.

20738-2 Paperbound $3.00

DUTCH-ENGLISH AND ENGLISH-DUTCH DICTIONARY
by F. Renier

For travel, literary, scientific, or business Dutch you will find this the most convenient, practical, and comprehensive dictionary on the market. It contains more than 60,000 entries, with full definitions, colloquialisms, shades of meaning, formal phrases, and idiomatic expressions. Compounds and technical terms are provided in both languages, and the complete conjugations of Dutch and English irregular and strong verbs are provided in separate lists. This is also the only dictionary in its size and price range that indicates the gender of nouns.

The new orthography adopted in 1947 is used throughout, but the old spellings are often indicated in the text. Accented syllables of each word are pointed out; plurals and parts of speech are identified throughout; and, finally, since the two halves have been independently compiled, reference from one half to the other will be found more than usually helpful.

588pp. 4¾ x 6½.   20224-0 Clothbound **$3.25**

PHONETICS

by Bertil Malmberg

Prepared by the Professor of Phonetics, Lund University, Sweden, this is the only full, detailed coverage of phonetics which is specific enough to be of practical value, yet simple and clear enough to be used by intelligent readers without previous training. It covers physical aspects of sound, physiological phonetics (or the actual production of sounds), special features (tone, stress, pitch), combinatory phonetics, phonemics, historical phonetics, evolution of sounds, linguistic geography and similar necessary topics. Professor Malmberg draws upon languages from all over the world, and provides thorough, specific analyses of English, French and German sound systems. As a result we recommend this book highly to anyone currently working with a foreign language; unless you have studied phonetics formally and thoroughly, it is certain to teach you much that is important to your foreign language study. Revised translation of 3rd French edition, enlarged with special material for English-speaking users. 63 illustrations. iv + 123pp. 5⅜ x 8½.

21024-3 Paperbound $1.25

ESSENTIALS OF RUSSIAN

by A. von Gronicka & H. Bates-Yakobson

Better than a record alone, better than a first-rate grammar alone, this is a superior language course that uses both a 400-page grammar and a 50-minute hi-fi LP to give you the best method of home study on the market today.

The grammar is a 400-page book published by Prentice-Hall, and now being used in scores of colleges and universities around the nation: Johns Hopkins, Dartmouth, Syracuse, Wisconsin, Texas, etc. 30 chapters contain functional reading exercises, vocabulary lists, questions, translations, and exercises. The record (prepared by the same authors to be used expressly with their grammar) begins with a complete review of every Russian sound and uses three speakers (in 12 conversational passages) to give you variety in voice types. A 44-page manual includes everything on the record and its English translations, which are as literal as possible in order to build your vocabulary more efficiently.

ESSENTIALS OF RUSSIAN text by A. von Gronicka and H. Bates-Yakobson. 400pp. 6 x 9. Clothbound. ESSENTIALS OF RUSSIAN record. 12″ 33⅓ rpm. MANUAL. 44pp. 5½ x 11½.   98831-7 The set, **$10.70**

Note: The record, with its manual, is completely self-contained, and may be used alone, or in conjunction with any other grammar.

Record, manual, jacket.   98830-9 The set, **$4.95**

CONVERSATIONAL CHINESE
by Morris Swadesh

Contrary to popular belief, Chinese grammar is really very simple. There are no elaborate conjugations or declensions, no multitudinous forms, and no difficult sound changes. Syntax is equally simple. Thus, you will be able to learn a surprising amount of colloquial Mandarin Chinese from this book, which was originally prepared for the United States Army.

Using a phonetic system that you can read at sight, Dr. Swadesh, one of America's foremost linguists, covers the most important, most useful speech patterns. Sounds, the system of tones, basic sentence structures, systems of negation, use of particles and similar essential material are all treated, with many helpful practice exercises based on everyday situations. At the end of the book is printed a 98-page English to Chinese dictionary, in which both individual words and ready-made sentences are given, with full indication of tones (an unusual feature for an elementary book). To make learning easier for you, Chinese characters and Chinese writing systems are not used in this book.

Formerly titled "Chinese in Your Pocket." xvi + 158pp.
21123-1 Paperbound **$1.50**

INVITATION TO SPANISH POETRY

edited by Eugenio Florit

This 12″ high fidelity recording contains 34 full poems—ballads, mystical verse, love poetry, sonnets, odes, folk poetry—and lengthy selections from three longer works. Ranging in time from the 12th century Cantar de Mío Cid to the middle 20th century, it contains work by Ruiz, Garcilaso de la Vega, Góngora, St. John of the Cross, Lope de Vega, Quevedo y Villegas, Bécquer, Unamuno, García Lorca, Jiménez, Hernández, Alberti and other great figures in Spanish poetry. Professor Florit of Columbia, himself one of the foremost modern Spanish poets, has selected and edited this material, and together with Mrs. Agostini de del Río reads it himself. Playing time is 47:13 minutes.

Accompanying the record is a full book containing Spanish texts recorded, faced by English translations, together with biographical and critical notes, and 24 portraits. As a result this is not only a scholarly work of great value, but a most useful set for listeners interested in Spanish culture.

Record. Book (150pp., 5⅜ x 8½). Album.
99894-0 The set **$4.95**

FRENCH—HOW TO SPEAK AND WRITE IT
by Joseph Lemaître

This is probably the most delightful, useful and comprehensive elementary book available for learning spoken and written French, either with or without a teacher. Working on the principle that a person learns more quickly by example than by rule, the author has put together a book that abounds in sparkling, colloquial French conversations on a wide variety of subjects, plus superb grammar, vocabulary and idiom studies presented through French sentences that demonstrate the language rather than merely describe it.

This book, though eminently useful for self study, is especially amenable to classroom use or study with a private tutor. The variety of teaching aids that this book places at the teacher's disposal is remarkable. Each lesson contains a dialogue, a section on grammar and idioms (replete with examples), and extensive practice exercises. In addition there are 13 double-page sketches of specific scenes (train station, beauty parlor, interior of a house) with pertinent items numbered and identified in French and English; sketches and photographs which the student is asked to describe in French; French sayings, quips, etc.

The dialogues encompass an exceptionally wide range of real-life situations, and are extended to include most of the basic vocabulary one would need in each situation. The appendices contain convenient tables of regular and irregular verbs, additional vocabulary, a section on letter writing and other useful material.

Index. Appendix. 400 illustrations. 403pp. 5⅜ x 8½.

20268-2   Paperbound **$3.00**

NEW RUSSIAN-ENGLISH AND ENGLISH-RUSSIAN DICTIONARY

by M. A. O'Brien

This thoroughly tested reference work provides an unusually comprehensive guide to the reading, speaking and writing of Russian for both beginning and advanced students. Over 70,000 entries are provided, with full information on accentuation and grammatical classifications. All important meanings are given under each word, with many idiomatic uses and colloquialisms. Irregular verbs are listed in tables, while individual entries indicate stems, transitiveness, perfective and imperfective aspects, conjugation, and both regular and irregular sound changes. Genders, sound changes, irregularities, plurals are indicated for nouns, while irregular adjectives are given in both positive and comparative forms. Prepositional entries indicate cases governed. This is one of the very few dictionaries where accent changes within the conjugation of verbs and the declension of nouns are fully indicated.

Other features include pronunciation, translations of first names and geographical terms. A conversion table analyzes older Russian non-metric weights and measurements, while a bibliography lists more specialized language aids.

Complete unabridged reproduction. 738pp. 4½ x 6⅜.

20208-9 Paperbound **$2.75**

A FOUNDATION DICTIONARY OF RUSSIAN

by B. Anpilogova and others

Prepared by a team of topnotch Russian linguists and educators, this book has been prepared specially for the English-speaker who is studying Russian. It consists of 3,000 highest frequency Russian words, carefully selected and analyzed according to submeanings. In addition to lexical and grammatical data, it also gives ready-made sentences and phrases for each word (in both English and Russian), illustrating exact idiomatic usage.

This dictionary is one of the handiest tools for a beginner or intermediate student in Russian studies. It is probably the only high semantic frequency list generally available for Russian, the only established list that will tell you which words you should know to have a basic Russian vocabulary. Since all this material is presented to you in sentence form, it is very easy to learn.

Formerly titled "Essential Russian-English Dictionary." 178pp. 5⅜ x 8.   21860-0 Paperbound **$1.50**

ESSENTIAL GRAMMARS

This unusual series has been devised to help adults with limited learning time, presenting fully and clearly basic colloquial forms and constructions. Enabling you to achieve communication in a remarkably short time, or to understand the material in phrase-approach record courses or books, these books stress explanation rather than rote memory; clarity of presentation; regularities rather than irregularities; many short cuts and ways to avoid constructions difficult for an English-speaker; modern presentation techniques, often more effective than traditional ones; reference to English parallels. These books are not baby talk or over simplifications, however they are thorough coverages without dead wood or archaic elements. Each volume also contains an appendix explaining grammatical terminology. The French and Spanish volumes contain lists of cognates (words nearly identical in form and meaning) for vocabulary building. All 5⅜ x 8.

ESSENTIAL GERMAN GRAMMAR, G. Stern, E. Bleiler. 128pp.
20422-7 **$1.25**

ESSENTIAL FRENCH GRAMMAR, S. Resnick. 159pp.
20419-7 **$1.25**

ESSENTIAL SPANISH GRAMMAR, S. Resnick. 128pp.
20780-3 **$1.25**

ESSENTIAL ITALIAN GRAMMAR, O. Ragusa. 111pp.
20779-X **$1.25**

ESSENTIAL JAPANESE GRAMMAR, E. Bleiler. 158pp.
21027-8 **$1.25**

ESSENTIAL PORTUGUESE GRAMMAR, A. Prista. 125pp.
21650-0 **$1.25**

INVITATION TO SPANISH POETRY

edited by Eugenio Florit

This 12″ high fidelity recording contains 34 full poems—
ballads, mystical verse, love poetry, sonnets, odes, folk
poetry—and lengthy selections from three longer works.
Ranging in time from the 12th century Cantar de Mío Cid
to the middle 20th century, it contains work by Ruiz,
Garcilaso de la Vega, Góngora, St. John of the Cross, Lope
de Vega, Quevedo y Villegas, Bécquer, Unamuno, García
Lorca, Jiménez, Hernández, Alberti and other great figures
in Spanish poetry. Professor Florit of Columbia, himself
one of the foremost modern Spanish poets, has selected
and edited this material, and together with Mrs. Agostini
de del Río reads it himself. Playing time is 47:13 minutes.

Accompanying the record is a full book containing Spanish
texts recorded, faced by English translations, together
with biographical and critical notes, and 24 portraits. As
a result this is not only a scholarly work of great value,
but a most useful set for listeners interested in Spanish
culture.

Record. Book (150pp., 5⅜ x 8½). Album.
99894-0 The set **$4.95**